KATHERINE
WANTS
·RANDY COOKS·

THE ULTIMATE DATE NIGHT
COOKBOOK

Randy Feltis &
Katherine Feltis

VICTORY BELT PUBLISHING INC.

Las Vegas

First published in 2025 by Victory Belt Publishing Inc.

ISBN-13: 978-1-628605-43-3

Brand manager and copywriter assistant: Shanley Gibb

Cover design: Kat Lannom

Interior design and illustrations: Yordan Terziev and Boryana Yordanova

Cover photo: Noah Campbell

Author photo: Jennifer Klementti

Food and lifestyle photography: Altomodo

Printed in Canada
TC 0125

CONTENTS

INTRODUCTION

OUR
LOVE STORY

Our love story began at a little restaurant called Oscar's. Randy was the chef/owner and Katherine was a bartender. For our first date, we went to Randy's condo for a movie night. He had a bottle of Veuve, M&Ms, shrimp cocktail, and oysters, and he put on *Fight Club*. Let's just say we didn't watch *Fight Club* until we got back together much later. It was flirtatious, hot, and spicy, but it didn't last very long because honestly, we were young and dumb. That's okay because as they say, what's meant to be will be.

Fast-forward fifteen years. We were both freshly divorced, living down the street from each other, and Katherine thought, I need to jump on this fast. So that's exactly what she did. She threw caution to the wind and slid into Randy's DMs on Instagram, asking him where in town he had his Range Rover serviced. It was, of course, a thinly veiled excuse to get back in contact, and luckily, it worked. He sent her the contact and asked if she needed a ride. We didn't want this opportunity to pass us by again; we were both ready and wanted the same thing. Just like that, our old flame rekindled hotter and stronger than ever.

From that initial outing to the mechanic, the fun was never-ending. We planned so many extravagant dates, including a spur-of-the-moment second date to Chicago for a culinary whirlwind, where we went on a romantic boat cruise complete with champagne and oysters (aka Katherine's love language). Next was a quick trip in NYC, where Le Bernardin became one of our favorite restaurants, and a romantic getaway in Barcelona, where we visited all of Katherine's go-to spots, including Bar Cañete. You'll notice that we call out this place time and time again in this cookbook because honestly, it's simply the best, and we've created so many memories there.

When COVID-19 hit, we had to get a little more creative when it came to keeping the romance alive. During lockdown, we decided to move into Randy's mid-century home. It seemed to be filled with emotional baggage from Randy's previous marriage, so we began our renovation journey—ordered bins and purged, painted the whole house white, and started digging up the old gardens once spring arrived. But that wasn't all we were doing!

As you may know, Randy is a chef, so he was cooking every meal for Katherine, every single day, no matter how crazy her request was, because lockdown was a time to indulge and make your own fun experiences. Then we thought, why not do meals virtually with our friends and family during the pandemic? So we held an online cooking class for Randy's brother's company's Christmas party and started sharing our recipes on Instagram. That got us thinking, how can we turn this into something? It blossomed into the brand most of you know and love, Katherine Wants.

We started filming all the recipes that Randy was cooking and putting them on TikTok and Instagram. The videos quickly took off, and our followers kept requesting more recipes and wanting to see what Katherine was going to ask for next. Since that initial video, we've shared thousands of recipes with over a million followers across our platforms, and they continue to grow like we never could've expected.

Apparently, Katherine Wants didn't keep us busy enough! In Randy's words, we said giddy up and decided to grow a tiny human—our daughter, Livvie. As the pandemic eased, we also opened Salty Blonde Bagel Bar, where Randy honed the menu and Katherine designed the look and feel of the joint, and together we made another tiny human!

Our love for sharing our relationship and food with our followers led us to this chapter in our lives: our debut cookbook. With this book, we wanted to romanticize date nights in for every occasion in a relationship, from first dates and meeting the parents to growing old together. This cookbook is filled with nostalgic favorites and familiar dishes that'll be by your side as you build out the chapters of your own love story. Plus, we've added in some love tips and tricks that we've learned along the way to help you through those common bumps in the road.

We hope you and your partner love this book as much as we do. Just remember that if you ever get into trouble, need an excuse to celebrate, or just want to show your partner you care, pink champagne and king crab go a long way. Or simply head to one of the chapters in this book and pick a recipe—it'll do the trick!

Love,

Katherine x Randy.

OUR LOVE STORY TIMELINE

We launched Katherine Wants.

We moved in together and blended our family.

We got engaged and decided to spend forever together!

2020
It was a year of personal and professional milestones, and lots of reasons to celebrate.

2019
We rekindled our relationship and our love story began. It was a year of travel and adventure.

2021

We took our first trip together to Chicago.

We fell in love in New York City.

We had our beautiful baby girl, Livvie.

We found our new favorite destination, Barcelona.

We built and opened
Salty Blonde Bagel Bar in
Barrie, Ontario.

We had our second beautiful
baby girl, Romee.

We completed the
manuscript and
photography for our first-
ever cookbook.

2022

2024 Another busy year.

FUTURE

2023 More milestones
and travel.

2025

Oh my stars!
The rest is yet to come!
Giddy up!

We got married!

We spent our honeymoon
in Spain.

KATHERINE
WANTS
·RANDY COOKS·

THE ULTIMATE DATE NIGHT
COOKBOOK

Randy Feltis & Katherine Feltis

Our debut cookbook was
published, just in time for
Valentine's Day!

ABOUT
THIS BOOK

Relationships aren't always linear—ours certainly wasn't!—and neither is this book. Normally, cookbooks group together similar recipes—for example, all soups or all chicken recipes are placed in the same chapter—and order the recipes according to the traditional sequence of appetizer to main course to dessert.

This cookbook is different. It is inspired by love, and the power of a delectable date night meal to impress a hoped-for partner in romance or to add a spark to a years-long marriage. So, while we agree there's a right way to begin and end an evening—our recipe collection does, after all, start off with our favorite cocktails and conclude with sweet indulgences—aside from that, it's up for grabs according to where you are in your love life.

Are you having the parents over for the first time and want to win them over? We've included a chapter of recipes to help you with that, ranging from elegant Prime Rib au Jus to a classic and comforting Three-Cheese Chicken Parmigiana, to put everyone at ease. Need to say "I'm sorry" to your sweetheart? The recipes in the "Get Out of Jail Free Card" chapter are designed to do just that. Just remember to prepare something they can't resist—that will melt their heart. For Katherine, a charcuterie board with a selection of cheeses and accoutrements and some wine usually does the job.

How about a lazy breakfast in bed on a Sunday morning? The "Morning Glory" chapter is filled with small touches designed to impress, like making your own coffee syrup or granola, as well as more elaborate breakfasts, like Nutella French Toast or the Ham and Brie Croissant Pudding. Want to do something special for your love but are pinched on time? See the "Quickies" chapter.

Starting at the beginning? Try the impressive dishes in the "First Date" chapter; they will wow your date, securing the second date before the meal is done. (Think Oysters Rockefeller, Beef Carpaccio, or a rich Cream of Mushroom Soup deglazed with whiskey.) Has your romance evolved into something sure and established? Then the "Going Steady" and "Growing Old Together" chapters might be for you. You'll find reliable classics that never get old, and that are so delicious you'll want to make them over and over again: Oysters Mignonette, Cheese Fondue, Spicy Vodka Penne, Boeuf Bourguignon, and Cauliflower Chicken Pot Pie, to name a few.

Wherever you are in the evolution of your romance, we want this book to be your go-to guide to success. In these pages, you'll find a hundred of our best recipes to help you celebrate every milestone in your relationship. But this is more than a cookbook. In addition to steal-their-heart recipes, we've included our best dating advice in the "Secret Sauce" section and have sprinkled Love Taps throughout the book.

The range of flavors and cooking styles in this cookbook is very broad, reflecting our tastes and lifestyle (which includes travel near and far whenever we can fit it in). There's not much we won't try, and we firmly believe that a little adventure keeps the spark alive. So you'll find lots of different dishes to suit any taste and any date.

Some of the recipes are inspired by dining out at our favorite local spots, or in far-flung spots like Bar Cañete in Barcelona. There's nothing more flattering to a chef than trying to recreate a delicious dish you had at a restaurant in your own kitchen, adding your personal twist. Others are family favorite recipes handed down to us. The Pernod Chicken, for example, is a recipe that Katherine's grandmother perfected.

While a handful of the recipes are Katherine's pride and joy, like the Lentil, Feta, and Parsley Salad, the majority are a result of Randy's experiments. He loves to take a perfectly fine recipe and mess with it to see if he can make it even better. Nine times out it ten, it gets worse—that's when basically everything goes to the bollocks. But that one time out of ten, it's magic. Those are the recipes we're sharing with you here, the best-of-our-best for meals that will impress your date (or spouse) and keep them coming back for more.

SOME TIPS
before YOU BEGIN

First and foremost, enjoy the process. Food made with love, and while you're having a good time, tastes better. It really does. So relax and savor the moment. And if part of the fun is taking a swig from the bottle of white that you're deglazing the pan with, have at it. It's a form of quality control, after all. Because the wine you cook with should always be drinkable.

Want to make your date nights really special? The Love Taps found below many of the recipes offer tips for taking the dish to the next level, and your romance along with it.

Be sure to review the "Kitchen and Pantry Date Night Staples" section beginning on page 21 to familiarize yourself with the range of tools we use and some of the staple ingredients we turn to again and again. You don't want to be caught off guard, lacking the right tool for the task at a critical moment. If you read the recipes carefully before you go shopping and before you start cooking to discover what fresh ingredients are needed, and to learn if there are components of the recipe that you can make ahead, you'll be more relaxed when your date arrives.

Most of the recipes in this book call for ingredients available at just about any grocery store, but a few use ingredients that may take a little more effort to procure, require an online purchase, and/or are a little pricey. White anchovies and caviar are two examples (see Oyster Shooter on page 45, Golden Beet Carpaccio on page 144, and Caviar Pizza Fritta on page 197). You can save these recipes for extra-special date nights. But we hope you do try these unique ingredients; they are what make the recipes that use them, and make the night.

Finally, if you'd like to look up recipes by more conventional categories, such as appetizers and soups, or by key ingredients, such as chicken, fish, eggs, and so forth, you can do that by using the index at the back of the book.

SECRET SAUCE: OUR RECIPE *for a* SUCCESSFUL RELATIONSHIP

Oh my stars! Relationships are both thrilling and challenging, but totally worth it in the end. The tricky thing is, no two relationships are the same, so there's no secret sauce that works for everyone. Sometimes you just have to take that leap, test out a new ingredient, try a different direction, and, if all else fails, follow your gut. That's exactly what we did both times around, and now here we are, with three kids and two restaurants (Farmhouse and Salty Blonde Bagel Bar), eager to spend the rest of our lives together.

Here is our dating advice, or recipe for a successful relationship, if you will. If you're still searching for that special someone, we hope you find your own Katherine or Randy!

Katherine's Dating Advice

PUT YOURSELF OUT THERE!

I jumped into Randy's DMs on Instagram as soon as I knew he was available. Next thing you know, we were on a date to the mechanic. What's meant to be will be, but not if you don't go after it.

BE YOURSELF.

I think this is so important when it comes to longevity in any relationship. Be genuine. It goes a long way.

RELAX.

I'm very aware of the control freak inside me. I really wanted us to finally be together, more than anything. But something about Randy's words and actions allowed me to feel calm and confident, and I was able to relax—a sure sign that this was meant to be. If the person you're into/seeing/investing time in doesn't give you a sense of calm, it's okay to walk away or check yourself.

COOK TOGETHER!

It's so nice to be wined and dined. A restaurant date will never get old, but the dynamic of cooking together is much more special. On one of our first dates, Randy made me scallop crudo, zucchini blossoms, and a latte decorated with 24-karat gold. Many of these early-day dating recipes have become go-to dishes that we like to prepare and enjoy together today. Your kitchen dynamic will be unique to you and your date, and it may evolve like the relationship does: for example, you might like to do most of the work in the kitchen, requesting a little sous chef assistance from time to time, or it might be more of a 50/50 split.

GET OUT *of* YOUR COMFORT ZONE.

Be open to new experiences and new foods. Be adventurous. This is why Randy and I love to travel. When we have a chance, we return to Spain and go to our favorite places, trying everything new on the menu. But travel isn't a prerequisite. A good local restaurant headed by an experimental chef who changes the menu regularly can supply you with new dishes and ingredients to try. Novelty keeps things fresh.

TALK *about* YOUR GOALS.

It's important to make sure you're aligned. Even if you don't have identical goals, expressing the aims that you have for yourself just might open your partner's eyes to something they hadn't considered. This was key for me because I knew I wanted to get married and have kids, so I needed to know Randy was open to this from the get-go.

ALWAYS HAVE *a* PLAN!

I've always written down a five-year and a ten-year plan. This is important, in my opinion, as an individual and as a couple. Everyone should do it. It's all about manifestation.

Randy's Dating Advice

YOUR PARTNER ALWAYS COMES FIRST.

It doesn't matter what you have going on. If you're not able to put your person first, it's never going to work. Trust me, I have experienced this firsthand.

OPEN *the* DOOR.

The tiniest gestures go a long way! The next time you're with your special someone, don't forget to open that door. Whether it's a car door or the door to a restaurant, open it up and show them you care.

BUY FLOWERS UNEXPECTEDLY.

Listen, anyone can buy flowers on Valentine's Day or an anniversary. Why not show them you're thinking of them by bringing home flowers on a random Wednesday? I pair them with some cava, and Katherine is a happy girl.

SHOW UP *with* CHEESE.

It's okay to be a little cheesy every once in a while. Especially if you show up with the good stuff. Surprise them with a little afternoon or late-night cheese delight. Katherine never says no to cheese.

CHAMPAGNE TASTES BETTER *on* MONDAYS.

Why not start the week off on a fantastic note with a glass of bubbles? Say cheers to the little things, because at the end of the day, life and relationships are hard. So celebrate the little wins.

SEND HER PICS.

Perhaps your special someone has a thing for vintage cars. Or maybe trees or cats. Whenever you run across what they love, take a pic and send it to them to show that they're on your mind. Listen, some guys like to send a different type of pic, but seeing as our love language is food, a good grocery pic of an oddball variety of broccoli or eggplant goes a long way for Katherine. Plus, it puts a smile on both of our faces. If you can't laugh together, what can you do?

DON'T OVERCOOK *the* EGGS.

The real secret is to never overcook anything, but let's start with eggs. No one wants to wake up to overcooked eggs. Properly cooking your breakfast will start both of your days off right—no yolks about it.

KITCHEN *and* PANTRY DATE NIGHT STAPLES

Listen, we've planned a date night or two in our lives, so we know how stressful it is. But it doesn't have to be. When it comes to planning the perfect date night in for that special someone, it all starts in the kitchen. This section provides a snapshot of our tried-and-true kitchen and pantry essentials that have given us our best dates to date. Whether you're hosting your first date or your fiftieth, make sure you have these items on hand to give them what they want! Once you have the staples, all you need to do is head out for the wonderfully fresh stuff—the "oh my stars" of the show: the produce, meat, seafood, dairy, eggs, and so on.

We've also listed some less-common tools and ingredients here. When an item is used in just one recipe in the book, we name the recipe that features it so you can decide whether you want to invest in that tool or make a special trip to the grocery store for it.

INGREDIENTS

FATS & OILS

Butter, unsalted

Extra-virgin olive oil (Terra Delyssa is our favorite brand)

Toasted sesame oil

NUTS & SEEDS

Almonds

Cashews

Flax seeds

Hazelnuts

Macadamia nuts

Pine nuts

Pistachios, raw as well as roasted and salted

Pumpkin seeds

Sunflower seeds

Walnuts

SPICES, DRIED HERBS & SEASONING BLENDS

Bay leaves

Black peppercorns

Cardamom pods

Chili powder

Cinnamon (ground, sticks)

Dry mustard (mild or moderately hot, such as Keen's; not Colman's)

Montreal steak spice

Nutmeg (ground)

Oregano leaves

Paprika (sweet and smoked)

Sumac

Vanilla (extract and beans)

White pepper (ground)

SALTS

Celery salt

Flaky black lava salt (for Frozen Avocado Margarita, page 42)

Flaky sea salt (such as Maldon)

Iodized salt

Kosher salt

FROZEN ITEMS

Green peas

Ice

Ice cream (store-bought or homemade, see page 228)

King crab legs

CANNED & BOTTLED GOODS

A.1. Sauce

Anchovies

Capers

Chili crisp (preferably Momofuku)

Coconut cream and milk

Cornichons

Dijon mustard (classic [smooth] and grainy)

Dill pickles

Fish sauce

Gherkins

Harissa

Hazelnut cocoa spread (Nutella is our favorite)

Hot sauce (Frank's RedHot Sauce [the original version] and Sriracha are our go-tos based on the heat level we're after; for extra-hot, we go for Tabasco)

Mayonnaise

Olives (green, black, Castelvetrano)

Peanut butter (smooth salted)

Smoked salmon caviar (for Oyster Shooter, page 45)

Soy sauce

Stock (beef, chicken, and vegetable)

Sturgeon caviar (for Caviar Pizza Fritta, page 197)

Sun-dried tomatoes (packed in oil)

Truffle aioli (for Beef Carpaccio, page 50)

Vinegars (red wine, white wine, distilled white, natural rice wine vinegar)

White anchovies (aka boquerones) (for Golden Beet Carpaccio, page 144)

White miso paste (for Oyster Shooter, page 45)

Whole peeled tomatoes (preferably San Marzano)

Worcestershire sauce

DRY GOODS

00 flour (aka pizza flour) (for Caviar Pizza Fritta, page 197)

All-purpose flour (unbleached)

Baking powder

Baking soda

Bread flour (unbleached)

Breadcrumbs, plain (panko and regular)

Coarse whole-wheat flour (for Irish Brown Soda Bread, page 218)

Cocoa powder

Cornstarch

Dates (pitted)

Dried black currants (aka zante currants or Corinth raisins)

Espresso beans (for Espresso Martini, page 37)

Pasta (Barilla is a good standby brand that is available at almost all grocery stores)

Rice (Arborio for risotto [see page 175] and long-grain as a staple)

Rolled oats (aka old-fashioned oats)

Yeast (active dry and instant)

SWEETENERS

1:1 simple syrup (for cocktails)

Maple syrup*

Molasses (such as Grandma's original unsulphured [or fancy in Canada])

Pure honey

Sugar (granulated, light and dark brown, powdered, and superfine)

We use a lot of maple syrup in our cooking and baking, and even in our cocktails. We're lucky to have a family connection in the sugaring business: Randy's dad has a sugar shack and supplies us with all we can use of the stuff, which we like to call "tree sauce." When sourcing maple syrup, make sure it's 100% pure.

WINE, STILL & SPARKLING (FOR DRINKING & COOKING)

Cava

Champagne (for an extra-special celebration; Katherine's current favorite is Laurent Perrier Rosé)

Marsala wine (for Brûléed Figs with Sabayon, page 231)

Prosecco

Red (pinot noir and Cabernet Sauvignon) (for Boeuf Bourguignon, page 171, and Red Wine–Braised Short Ribs, page 179)

Riesling (for Vanilla Poached Pear, page 194)

Rosé (dry) (Hampton Water has been our go-to lately)

White (Sauvignon Blanc or other crisp dry white)

DISTILLED SPIRITS & LIQUEURS (FOR DRINKING & COOKING)

Amaro (for Espresso Martini, page 37)

Armagnac (for Creamy Peppercorn Sauce, page 225; or substitute brandy)

Blanco (silver) tequila

Brandy

Coconut-infused tequila (for Frozen Avocado Margarita, page 42)

Coffee liqueur (for Espresso Martini, page 37)

Cognac (for French Onion Soup, page 193)

Dark rum (for Tiramisu, page 247)

Kirsch (for Cheese Fondue, page 140)

Limoncello (for Limoncello Mint Spritz, page 29)

Orange liqueur (for Frozen Avocado Margarita, page 42)

Pernod

Pimm's No. 1 (for The Pimm's Cup, page 30)

Vodka

Whiskey (for Cream of Mushroom Soup, page 61)

EQUIPMENT

PREP TOOLS

Blender (we prefer Vitamix, but a high-powered blender is not required)

Box grater

Bread knife

Butcher twine

Chef's knife

Colander

Fine-mesh sieve

Food processor

Immersion blender (or substitute a countertop blender)

Julienne peeler (for The Pimm's Cup, page 30)

Mandoline (for Ten-Vegetable Slaw, page 152)

Microplane zester

Oyster knife

Paring knife

Pepper mill

Stand mixer (we prefer KitchenAid or SMEG)

Sturdy wooden cutting board

Vegetable peeler

COOKING TOOLS

Braiser, large (or substitute a deep-sided cast-iron frying pan)

Cast-iron frying pans—medium (9- or 10-inch) and large (11- or 12-inch)

Deep-fry thermometer

Dutch oven, large (8- to 9-quart)

Fish spatula (optional; for Coconut Poached Cod, page 132)

Heavy-bottomed frying pans—small (8-inch), medium (9- or 10-inch), and large (11- or 12-inch) (we prefer All-Clad)

Heavy-bottomed pots of various sizes (we prefer All-Clad)

Kitchen blowtorch

Meat thermometer

Nonstick frying pans—medium (9- or 10-inch) and large (11- or 12-inch) (we prefer HexClad)

Roasting pan

Saucepans—small (2 to 4 cups), medium (1 to 2 quarts), and large (4 quarts)

Sauté pan

Soup ladle

Soup pot

Spatulas (rubber and metal)

Steamer basket (for Charred Octopus, page 135)

Stockpot

Whisk

Wooden spoons

BAKING TOOLS

Baking dishes of various sizes

Baking pan (9 by 13-inch)

Baking sheets

Bench knife

Loaf pan (5 by 9-inch)

Measuring cups, liquid and dry

Measuring spoons

Metal bowls of various sizes

Parchment paper

Pie pan (9-inch)

Pie weights (can substitute dried beans)

Ring molds (3-inch)

Rolling pin

Sheet pans (18 by 13 by 1 inch)

Springform pans (9-inch by 3-inch-deep and 12-inch)

Tart pan with removable bottom (12-inch)

Wire rack

GRILLING & SMOKING TOOLS

Charcoal grill (we prefer Napoleon)

Grilling tongs

High-quality/insulated gas grill (we prefer Napoleon)

Smoker or smoke box accessory that works with a grill

Wood chips

MISCELLANEOUS

18-ounce pump-action dispenser (for Vanilla Coffee Syrup, page 69)

Ice cream maker (for Vanilla Bean Soft-Serve, page 228)

COCKTAIL TOOLS & GLASSWARE

Cocktail shaker

Collins glasses

Coupe or cocktail glasses of various sizes (12, 8, and 6 ounces)

Flute glasses (8 ounces) (or substitute coupe glasses)

Ice cube tray

Long spoon, for stirring

Rocks glasses (12 ounces)

Shot glasses (2 ounces)

Tall glasses (14 ounces)

Wine bottle opener

Wine glasses of various sizes (16, 14, and 12 ounces)

Wooden muddler

TABLE SETTING & SERVING ESSENTIALS

Candles

Charcuterie board

Cheese knives

Demitasse spoons

Egg cups

Meat carving fork and knife

Mini bowls

Quality cutlery

Quality dishware (we like Viceroy & Boch)

Serving bowls and plates

Serving tools

Tabletop wine chiller

Wine glasses (for red, white, and sparkling)

BREAK
THE ICE

Toast the start of your new relationship with
these tasty cocktails

LIMONCELLO MINT SPRITZ

YIELD: 1 SERVING · PREP TIME: 1 MINUTE

It's never too soon for a trip to Italy. If you whip up this spritz for your date, you don't even need a passport! With one sip, you'll instantly be transported to the Italian countryside. With the second sip, you'll be planning your next date.

Ice

3 slices lemon

1½ ounces limoncello

¼ ounce fresh lemon juice

3 ounces chilled prosecco

2 ounces chilled soda water

1 handful fresh mint

1. Fill a 14-ounce white wine glass with ice and slip in the lemon slices, nestling them against the glass. Pour in the chilled limoncello and lemon juice, then top with the chilled prosecco and soda water. Give it a stir with a long spoon.

2. Slap the mint for extra fragrance before inserting it in the glass as a garnish.

For extra love, make your own limoncello. All you have to do is zest 12 very clean lemons, add 1½ cups of sugar, and top with 2 cups of 98-proof alcohol, such as vodka. Store it in a 2-quart airtight glass container in a cool, dark room for 3 months. Add 6 cups of filtered water, then strain into a clean 2-quart glass container and enjoy.

The PIMM'S CUP

YIELD: 1 SERVING · PREP TIME: 4 MINUTES

Nothing breaks the ice fast like a Pimm's Cup. This quickly became one of Katherine's favorite cocktails after she started watching *Vanderpump Rules*—it's one of their signature drinks. It pairs perfectly with binge watching, and watching your date's favorite reality show is much easier when you have one in hand.

1 long cucumber ribbon

3 large ice cubes

3 slices clementine

3 blackberries

3 raspberries

½ ounce fresh lemon juice

2 ounces Pimm's No. 1

4 ounces ginger ale

1 handful fresh mint

1. Lay the cucumber ribbon down the inside of a tall 14-ounce glass and fill the glass with the ice (try not to knock down the cucumber).

2. Add the clementine slices, blackberries, raspberries, lemon juice, Pimm's, and ginger ale. Gently stir the drink.

3. Slap the mint for extra fragrance before inserting it in the glass as a garnish.

Prep the cucumber ribbon ahead because it takes a little extra time, but the look is well worth the extra effort. The best tool to use to get a nice broad ribbon is a julienne peeler, but a regular vegetable peeler will also work. For long ribbons, use an English cucumber, which also has the benefit of being seedless (who wants cucumber seeds floating in their drink?). The classic glassware for this drink is a Collins glass, but a highball glass is fine too.

CILANTRO JALAPEÑO
MAPLE TEQUILA
on the ROCKS

YIELD: 1 SERVING · PREP TIME: 5 MINUTES

A little background for you: Randy's family has a sugar shack, so we're always adding maple syrup to our favorite cocktails to give them that familiar touch. It's a great replacement for simple syrup. For your first date, why not break the ice with a trip to a local farmers market or go to a sugar shack and get some maple syrup to take home to whip up this cocktail? You get two dates for the price of one! (If you don't live where maple syrup is produced, then how about an outing together to the liquor store to let your date pick out their favorite tequila?)

5 lime wedges

2 tablespoons fresh cilantro leaves

4 thin slices jalapeño pepper

½ ounce maple syrup

8 medium ice cubes

2 ounces blanco (silver) tequila

3 ounces soda water

FOR GARNISH:

2 sprigs fresh cilantro

⅛ teaspoon ground black pepper

SPECIAL EQUIPMENT:

12-ounce rocks glass

Cocktail shaker

1. Place a 12-ounce rocks glass in the freezer to chill.

2. In a cocktail shaker, muddle the lime wedges with the cilantro leaves and jalapeño slices. Add the maple syrup, ice, and tequila. Shake it vigorously, then shake it some more. Yes, it will dilute the drink a little, but a little water opens up the flavor of liquor.

3. Pour into the chilled rocks glass and top with the soda. Garnish with the cilantro sprigs and black pepper.

When you balance the lime perfectly with maple syrup, something magical happens. After shaking the cocktail, taste and adjust accordingly for that ideal balance, if needed. But be very careful—this one is dangerously delicious.

KATHERINE'S CAESAR

YIELD: 1 SERVING · PREP TIME: 2 MINUTES

There's no better way to ease into a first date than with a tasty Caesar, the Canadian version of a Bloody Mary. Katherine started making this cocktail for Randy when we first started dating. Before we had kids, we would each have one on Saturday and Sunday mornings. Now, with the kids running around, we tend to start the weekend days off with two.

RIMMER:

1 small lemon wedge

1 tablespoon celery salt

1 tablespoon Montreal steak spice

6 medium ice cubes

½ ounce fresh lemon juice

1½ teaspoons Worcestershire sauce

¼ teaspoon hot sauce, such as Tabasco for more heat or Frank's for a milder flavor

1 ounce olive brine

½ ounce pickle brine

2 ounces vodka

4 ounces Clamato juice

FOR GARNISH:

Pinch of kosher salt

3 pitted Castelvetrano olives

1 jumbo shrimp, cooked and peeled

1. Rim the glass: Lightly squeeze the lemon wedge, then wipe the wedge along the outside of the rim of a tall 14-ounce glass. On a saucer or other small plate, mix together the celery salt and Montreal steak spice. Roll the glass in the rimmer mixture.

2. Drop the ice into the rimmed glass, followed by the lemon juice, Worcestershire, hot sauce, olive brine, pickle brine, vodka, and Clamato juice and stir with a long spoon.

3. Garnish with a pinch of kosher salt, the olives, and a shrimp.

Acidity is the key to a proper Canadian Caesar. Yes, we do love the flavor of clam juice, but it's the acidity in the lemon juice and olive and pickle brines that pairs perfectly with the Clamato juice and makes for the perfect Caesar.

ESPRESSO MARTINI

YIELD: 1 SERVING · PREP TIME: 2 MINUTES

If you and your date are coffee lovers, then you need to serve up some espresso martinis. This martini has become a classic and a Katherine Wants fan favorite. So, sip on these and "espresso" yourself to your date.

1½ ounces chilled espresso

1½ ounces coffee liqueur

1½ ounces vodka

¾ ounce amaro

6 small ice cubes

3 espresso beans, for garnish

1. Place a 12-ounce wine glass, coupe, or cocktail glass in the freezer to chill.

2. Put all the ingredients, except the espresso beans, in a blender and blitz on high speed until completely smooth. This will give you a thick foamy head that will remain through the last sip.

3. Pour into the chilled glass and garnish with the espresso beans.

Amaro is an Italian liqueur that has a bittersweet herbal flavor profile. We like the voluptuous body it adds to a coffee martini.

To prep ahead of time, pour the first four ingredients into a blender jar and chill in the fridge. Feel free to multiply. When ready to serve, blend with the ice and garnish as described above.

FROZEN PEACH BELLINI

YIELD: 2 TO 4 SERVINGS
PREP TIME: 12 MINUTES, PLUS OVERNIGHT TO FREEZE PEACH MIXTURE

A first date is a cause for celebration—and so is peach season. Why not celebrate with a delicious, peachy, and bubbly Bellini? It's the perfect cocktail to start a new relationship on a refreshing note.

1½ ripe peaches, pitted

4 cherries, pitted

Juice of 1 lime

4 ounces water

2 (187-ml) bottles prosecco or Champagne, chilled

2 to 4 cherries with stems, for garnish

1. Toss the peaches and cherries in a blender, then add the lime juice and water and blend until smooth. Pour the fruit puree into a 5 by 9-inch loaf pan and freeze overnight.

2. Place two to four 8-ounce coupe or flute glasses in the freezer to chill.

3. Scrape the frozen fruit mixture with a fork to create peach-cherry snow and spoon into the frozen coupes. Top with the bubbles and garnish with a cherry.

We like to add cherries to our Bellinis; the blush of color and added tartness makes the drink extra-special and romantic.

If you like your drink a little sweeter, feel free to add 2 tablespoons of sugar to the blended fruit. Also, if you don't use all the frozen mixture, you can wrap it and keep it in the freezer for up to 2 weeks.

PEAR *and* PLUM WHITE SANGRIA

YIELD: 1 SERVING · PREP TIME: 2 MINUTES

Pears and plums are underrated, but when combined in this striking new twist on sangria, they are so refreshing. Talk about a lasting first impression! You can even pass this off as your own creation; we won't tell.

5 medium ice cubes

5 slices pear

5 slices plum

½ ounce orange liqueur

5 ounces crisp dry white wine, preferably Sauvignon Blanc, chilled

2 ounces sparkling water, chilled

1. Place the ice in a large wine glass (at least 16 ounces); we prefer to use stemless glasses for sangria, but stemmed glasses will work, too.

2. Lay the fruit in the glass, on top of the ice, then pour in the orange liqueur. Top with the white wine and sparkling water, then stir.

Looking to enjoy your favorite wine but with a kick? Sangria is your answer. Often, the fortifying element is brandy, but here we're using orange liqueur. This is your answer when the summer heat hits and you need a little extra chill and flavor. Don't be afraid to make this in larger batches and garnish along the way.

FROZEN AVOCADO MARGARITA

YIELD: 1 SERVING · PREP TIME: 3 MINUTES

We first discovered this game-changing margarita flavor during the pandemic. We'd had way too many avocados delivered, so we decided to throw them in the blender and turned them into this delicious cocktail. The avocado gives the margarita a velvety texture, and the coconut-infused tequila gives it a tropical feel. Why not pull the blender out for your date and make your own Margaritaville at home? It'll be a fiesta to remember.

¼ ripe avocado

1½ ounces blanco (silver) tequila

½ ounce orange liqueur

¼ ounce coconut-infused tequila

¾ ounce fresh lime juice

⅓ ounce simple syrup

6 medium ice cubes

FOR GARNISH:

1 slice avocado

⅛ teaspoon flaky black lava salt

1. Put all the ingredients in a blender and blend until smooth. Pour into a 6-ounce coupe or cocktail glass.

2. Sprinkle the slice of avocado with the black lava salt and garnish the drink.

We like to sprinkle the avocado garnish with black lava salt because the black color is so striking against the green, but any flaky salt will do.

OYSTER SHOOTER

YIELD: 6 SERVINGS · PREP TIME: 10 MINUTES

When it comes to dating, you have to give it your best shot from the get-go.
This shooter will do just that! It's fun, builds excitement, and is ultimately
a great way to start off your date.

6 oysters, freshly shucked (oyster liquor reserved)

3 medium ice cubes

3 ounces tomato juice

¼ ounce fresh lemon juice

¼ teaspoon white miso paste

¼ teaspoon hot sauce, such as Tabasco for more heat or Frank's for a milder flavor

4 ounces vodka

FOR GARNISH:

6 quail egg yolks (optional)

1 tablespoon finely diced cucumber

1 tablespoon seeded and finely diced jalapeño pepper

2 tablespoons smoked salmon caviar

1 tablespoon chopped fresh dill

SPECIAL EQUIPMENT:

2-ounce shot glasses

1. Place one shucked oyster and its liquor in each shot glass.

2. Put the ice, tomato juice, lemon juice, miso paste, hot sauce, and vodka in a cocktail shaker. Shake aggressively. Pour the strained mixture over the oysters, then add one quail egg yolk, if using, to each shot glass.

3. Evenly garnish the shots with the cucumber, jalapeño, caviar, and dill.

These shots are a bit of a pain to build, so make them up to 2 hours before your date arrives. Just slide a toothpick down the side of the glass to make sure some liquid gets beneath the oyster. This will ensure you get the slide you're looking for when you throw the shot back. For these shooters, you'll need 2-ounce shot glasses (aka double shot glasses). Standard shot glasses have a capacity of about 1½ ounces, which just isn't large enough to impress your date.

Also note that you'll be eating raw eggs here. If you're not comfortable with that, just leave them out. But they really do add a special touch!

FIRST
DATE

Dishes that'll wow your date so much,
they'll be asking for a second date before
they're done eating

OYSTERS ROCKEFELLER
· 49 ·

BEEF CARPACCIO
· 50 ·

SEARED SEA SCALLOPS
with CELERIAC PUREE
and CRISPY GUANCIALE
· 53 ·

BURRATA ARANCINI
· 54 ·

BEET-CURED GRAVLAX
· 57 ·

CURLY ENDIVE *and* APPLE
SALAD *with* GOAT CHEESE
CRÈME BRÛLÉE
· 58 ·

CREAM *of* MUSHROOM SOUP
· 61 ·

CRISPY ROSEMARY
CHICKEN WINGS
with HONEY HOT SAUCE
· 62 ·

GREEN COCONUT CURRY MUSSELS
· 65 ·

OYSTERS ROCKEFELLER

YIELD: 2 SERVINGS · PREP TIME: 20 MINUTES · COOK TIME: 12 MINUTES

Oysters have always been one of our favorite date night meals. On our first trip to Chicago, we took a private river cruise that was complete with bubbles and oysters Rockefeller, so they hold a special place in our hearts. Plus, this preparation is the perfect way to introduce oysters to a first-timer because they are milder when cooked, which makes them less intimidating. We guarantee your date or partner will quickly become obsessed with them.

BREADCRUMB TOPPING:

½ cup panko breadcrumbs

1 cup fresh parsley leaves

3 sprigs fresh dill

1 green onion, cut into thirds

1 tablespoon unsalted butter

3 tablespoons grated Asiago cheese

½ teaspoon kosher salt

½ teaspoon ground black pepper

1 tablespoon unsalted butter

2 cloves garlic, sliced

1 bunch spinach, washed

¼ teaspoon kosher salt

1 tablespoon Pernod

12 medium or large oysters, freshly shucked (oyster liquor reserved)

¼ lemon

SPECIAL EQUIPMENT:

Oyster knife (optional)

1. In a blender, pulse all the ingredients for the breadcrumb topping until they come together into a doughlike paste. Set aside.

2. In a medium cast-iron frying pan, melt the butter over medium heat. Add the garlic and sauté until soft. Toss in the spinach, season with the salt, and sauté until beginning to wilt. Deglaze with the Pernod and continue to cook until the spinach is completely wilted. Set aside.

3. Have an oven rack in the top position and turn the oven broiler on high. Sprinkle kosher salt on a sheet pan in two rows, about 1 inch deep; this will serve as a bed for the oyster shells to help them stay upright.

4. To assemble, remove the oysters from their shells, leaving the juice in the shells. Place six of the shells on one row of salt and the other six shells on the other row of salt. Evenly divide the sautéed spinach among the shells, then return the oysters to their shells. Scoop up about 1 tablespoon of the breadcrumb topping and press between your hands into a thin blanket to completely cover the oyster. Place on top of an oyster, then repeat with the rest of the topping mixture until all the oysters are topped with the paste.

5. Broil for 8 minutes, or until golden brown. Squeeze the lemon over the top and serve.

If you are unsure about shucking, ask your fishmonger to shuck the oysters for you and keep the oyster liquor. This can be done up to 4 days in advance.

BEEF CARPACCIO

YIELD: 2 SERVINGS · PREP TIME: 8 MINUTES

If you follow us on social media, you know that we love traveling to Miami. Every time we go there, we have to pop into our favorite restaurant, Carbone, and order the beef carpaccio. Since we don't visit Miami as often as we'd like, Randy put his own spin on the Carbone's dish that we love, and it quickly became a date night favorite for us. It's the perfect appetizer to share as you get to know each other.

3 tablespoons extra-virgin olive oil, divided

6 ounces beef tenderloin, thinly sliced

2 tablespoons truffle aioli

2 tablespoons finely crumbled toasted walnuts

1 tablespoon finely chopped shallots

1 tablespoon chopped fresh chives

1 handful arugula

6 button mushrooms, thinly sliced

½ teaspoon kosher salt

¼ teaspoon ground black pepper

Juice of ½ lemon

2 tablespoons grated Parmigiano-Reggiano cheese

1. Have on hand a 10- to 12-inch round platter or an oval platter of similar size.

2. Drizzle 1 tablespoon of the olive oil on a 14-inch piece of parchment paper. Arrange the sliced beef tenderloin on the parchment in a single layer, cover with another sheet of parchment, and bang the beef with a meat tenderizer or wine bottle until it's about 1/16 inch thick. Then, using a rolling pin, roll it out thinner yet into a rough circular or oval shape slightly larger than your platter. Place the platter on top of the parchment paper and trace an outline of the platter on the paper. Using kitchen scissors, cut the parchment paper and beef into the shape of the circle or oval. Remove the top layer of paper and flip the meat over onto the platter. (Save the excess meat you've trimmed for another use; a tartare or martini garnish would be great.)

3. Paint the meat with 1 tablespoon of the olive oil and the aioli, then top with the walnuts, shallots, chives, arugula, and mushrooms.

4. Finish with the salt, pepper, remaining tablespoon of olive oil, lemon juice, and Parmigiano-Reggiano.

Don't be afraid to overdress this dish. Lean raw beef needs lots of fat and acidity.

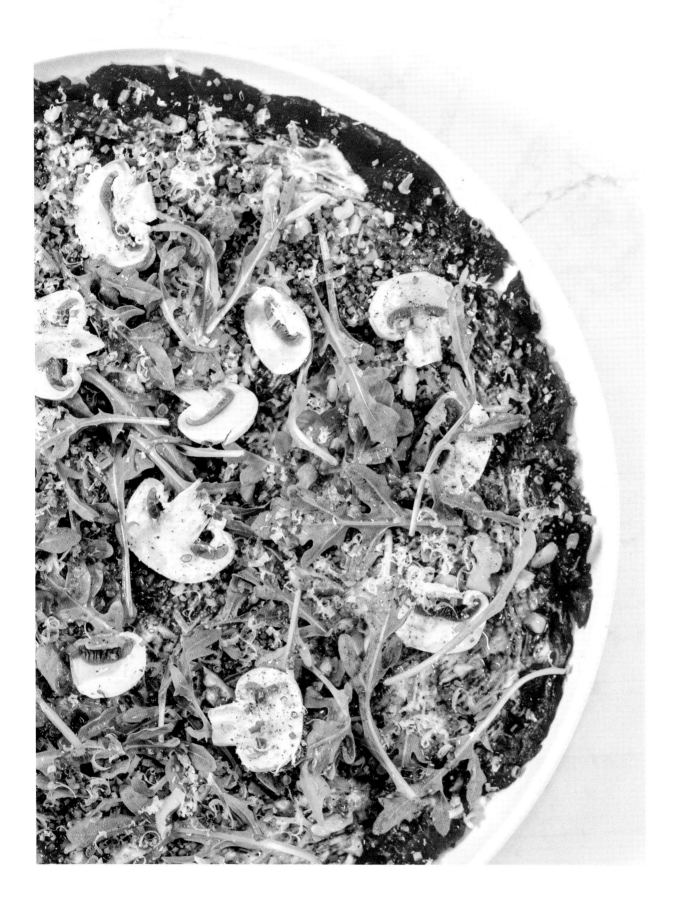

SEARED SEA SCALLOPS *with* CELERIAC PUREE *and* CRISPY GUANCIALE

YIELD: 2 SERVINGS · PREP TIME: 10 MINUTES · COOK TIME: 12 MINUTES

Nothing says romance like a delicious seafood dinner. If you are looking to really impress your date, these seared scallops are the way to go. The marriage of flavors in this dish is unforgettable and will definitely secure you that second date. But we'll let you "sea" for yourself.

CELERIAC PUREE:
(MAKES 2 CUPS)

1 small (8- to 12-ounce) celeriac (aka celery root), peeled and diced

1 apple, peeled and diced

2 cups milk

1 clove garlic, halved

2 tablespoons unsalted butter

1 teaspoon kosher salt

3 ounces guanciale or pancetta, cut into matchsticks (about 1 cup)

6 dry-packed sea scallops (U10/20 size), "feet" removed

1 teaspoon kosher salt

1 tablespoon extra-virgin olive oil

1 tablespoon pine nuts, toasted

1/8 teaspoon ground black pepper

1. Make the celeriac puree: Put all the ingredients in a small saucepan over medium heat. Bring to a gentle simmer, then cover and continue to simmer for about 10 minutes. When the celeriac is tender, transfer the contents of the pan to a blender and puree until smooth. Adjust the seasoning if needed.

2. Place the guanciale in a small frying pan along with a splash of water. Over medium heat, render the fat as the water evaporates. Continue cooking until the desired crispness, then remove with a slotted spoon and set aside.

3. Preheat a 12-inch cast-iron frying pan over medium heat.

4. Meanwhile, dry off the scallops on some paper towels and season with the salt.

5. When the pan is very hot, pour in the olive oil. You'll know the oil is hot enough if it smokes a little. Gently place the scallops in the hot oil and do not touch until a crust appears on the bottom edge, 2 to 3 minutes. Give a flip and repeat. Remove to a plate and let rest for 2 minutes.

6. To serve, spoon 1/4 cup of the celeriac puree into a small pasta bowl and top with three scallops and half of the crispy guanciale. Garnish with half of the toasted pine nuts and pepper. Repeat to make a second serving.

To get a proper sear on your scallops, make sure you dry them very well with a paper towel and have your pan good and hot.

BURRATA ARANCINI

YIELD: 2 TO 4 SERVINGS · PREP TIME: 10 MINUTES · COOK TIME: 5 MINUTES

Looking to ease those first-date jitters? These burrata arancini will do just that! Split them between you and bond over their deliciousness. Just make sure to let your date have the last one. Or, even better, if you don't finish them, store them in the fridge and reheat for your next date.

1½ cups plain breadcrumbs

1 teaspoon dried oregano leaves

1 teaspoon kosher salt

½ teaspoon ground black pepper

1 cup all-purpose flour

2 large eggs, beaten

3 cups leftover risotto (see page 175)

1 (4-ounce) ball burrata, chopped

12 paper-thin slices pancetta

6 cups vegetable oil, for frying

1 cup tomato sauce

4 fresh basil leaves

½ cup grated Parmigiano-Reggiano cheese

SPECIAL EQUIPMENT:

Deep-fry thermometer

1. Preheat the oven to 375°F and line a sheet pan with parchment paper.

2. Season the breadcrumbs with oregano, salt, and pepper. Set up the flour, seasoned breadcrumbs, and beaten eggs in three separate bowls to create a breading station.

3. Scoop up ¾ cup of the cooked risotto and spread it into a thin layer in the palm of your hand.

4. Place a tablespoon of the chopped burrata in the middle of the risotto and wrap the rice around the burrata to enclose it, then roll it into a ball. Roll the ball in the flour, then in the egg wash and seasoned breadcrumbs. Repeat to make a total of four balls.

5. Bake the pancetta on the prepared pan until shattering crisp, 9 to 12 minutes. Remove from the oven and set aside.

6. In a large saucepan over medium heat, preheat the vegetable oil to 375°F. (The oil should come no more than about halfway up the sides of the pan; if the oil level is higher than that, use a deeper pot, such as a stockpot.) Fry the arancini until crispy and golden, 3 to 4 minutes. When done, remove from the oil with a slotted spoon.

7. While the arancini are frying, warm the tomato sauce.

8. To serve, spoon ¼ cup of the tomato sauce onto a serving plate. Top with a rice ball, three slices of pancetta, a basil leaf, and a couple tablespoons of Parmigiano-Reggiano.

Make sure the balls are completely coated in the breading to protect the burrata. This allows them to be crisp on the outside and tender on the inside. It also creates the perfect cheese pull.

BEET-CURED GRAVLAX

YIELD: 4 TO 8 SERVINGS · PREP TIME: 10 MINUTES, PLUS 24 HOURS TO CURE

This dish is a stunning presentation of fish. Although it may come off as challenging, it's actually one of the easiest recipes in this entire book. It's definitely a game changer on a first date because it's dressed to impress and shows your date that you're willing to put in the effort. Just make sure to plan ahead, and if you don't finish it all, you can cover leftovers with plastic wrap and place in the coldest part of the fridge for up to a week.

CURING MARINADE:

¾ cup kosher salt

½ cup granulated sugar

1 cup shredded beet

1 ounce gin

¼ cup fresh dill fronds, chopped

Grated zest and juice of 1 orange

1½ pounds salmon, center-cut fillet, pin bones removed

½ cup crème fraîche

1 handful baby red Swiss chard

1. Place all the ingredients for the curing marinade in a large zip-top plastic bag.

2. Toss aggressively to blend well, then place the salmon fillet in the bag. Try to get all the air out, then seal and place it in the fridge with something heavy on top, like a carton of milk. Flip before bed and let it cure for 24 hours.

3. Remove and rinse off the curing marinade. Pat dry and slice ¼ inch thick.

4. Serve with the crème fraîche and Swiss chard.

Be sure to ask your fishmonger for very fresh salmon, and have them remove the pin bones and scales.

If you can't find baby red Swiss chard, you can substitute fresh dill sprigs.

CURLY ENDIVE *and* APPLE SALAD *with* GOAT CHEESE CRÈME BRÛLÉE

YIELD: 2 SERVINGS · PREP TIME: 8 MINUTES, PLUS 10 MINUTES TO FREEZE

This salad is a classic from Randy's previous restaurant, Oscar's. It was one of the bestsellers on the menu and was always recommended to the couples who walked through the door because it's great to share, and the sweet, salty creaminess was to die for. Don't let it fool you. It may scream 1999, but it really does slap. So, for your next first date, make sure to include this salad on the menu. You won't regret it.

GOAT CHEESE CRÈME BRÛLÉE:

1 (8-ounce) log fresh (soft) goat cheese

1 tablespoon granulated sugar

SALAD:

1 sweet apple, such as Honeycrisp, Ambrosia, or Fuji

2 cups torn curly endive (aka frisée or chicory)

3 tablespoons extra-virgin olive oil

Juice of ½ lemon

1 teaspoon kosher salt

½ teaspoon ground black pepper

SPECIAL EQUIPMENT:

2 (3-inch) ring molds

Kitchen torch (optional)

1. Divide the goat cheese evenly between the ring molds by packing it in firmly to make two cheese pucks. Chill the pucks in the freezer for 10 minutes.

2. Meanwhile, prepare the salad: Cut the apple into matchsticks and toss with the curly endive, olive oil, lemon juice, salt, and pepper. Taste and adjust the seasoning if needed, then divide between two plates.

3. Remove the goat cheese pucks from the freezer and slide them out of the ring molds. Sprinkle them with the sugar and torch until caramelized (brown is good, black is bad).

4. To serve, place the brûléed goat cheese pucks on top of the salads.

A kitchen torch will really help with the preparation of this dish. If you don't have one, place them in the oven to broil on high or until caramelized. We prefer Celebrity goat cheese. It's a Canadian brand made with 100% pure goat's milk. Look for the best fresh goat's milk cheese you can find in your area.

CREAM *of* MUSHROOM SOUP

YIELD: 8 TO 12 SERVINGS · PREP TIME: 15 MINUTES · COOK TIME: 55 MINUTES

They say it takes a kind heart to make a good soup. So, if you have a first date around the corner, take on this simple classic and show your date what you're all about. Plus, you can store the leftovers in the fridge for up to 5 days for your future dates.

2 tablespoons extra-virgin olive oil, plus extra for garnish

1 tablespoon unsalted butter

1 white onion, diced

2 cloves garlic, chopped

64 ounces mixed mushrooms (such as button, oyster, shiitake, and/or chanterelle), sliced (about 4 cups)

2 teaspoons fresh thyme leaves

1 teaspoon kosher salt

½ teaspoon ground black pepper

3 ounces whiskey

10½ cups chicken or vegetable stock

1 cup heavy cream, plus extra for garnish

½ cup croutons, for garnish

2 tablespoons thinly sliced fresh chives (aka Randy's 1,000 chives), for garnish

1. Heat the oil and butter in a stockpot over medium heat. Add the onion and sauté until transparent, about 8 minutes. Add the garlic, mushrooms, thyme, salt, and pepper and stir; allow the mushrooms to cook down and release their moisture, about 4 minutes. Be sure to stir frequently. When you see some color forming on the bottom of the pot, deglaze with the whiskey and scrape the bottom of the pot. Allow to cook until the liquid is reduced by half.

2. Pour in the stock and cream and simmer softly for 30 minutes, or until the mushrooms are soft. Blend one-third of the soup until smooth, then return it to the pot. Adjust the seasoning if needed.

3. Serve garnished with the croutons, a drizzle of cream and olive oil, and a sprinkling of chives.

Fresh mushrooms contain a lot of water, so cooking them down concentrates and builds some flavor, as does deglazing them with your favorite whiskey.

CRISPY ROSEMARY CHICKEN WINGS *with* HONEY HOT SAUCE

YIELD: 2 SERVINGS AS A MAIN COURSE, OR 4 SERVINGS AS AN APPETIZER
PREP TIME: 5 MINUTES · COOK TIME: 24 MINUTES

Why not wing it on your first date and get a little messy? These crispy, sweet and spicy wings are packed with flavor in every bite. Just make sure to ask your date if they prefer flats or drumettes so you can customize the dish to their liking. A little effort goes a long way! Plus, once they test out these wings, you'll know if they're a keeper.

WINGS:

⅓ cup plain breadcrumbs

2 tablespoons grated Parmigiano-Reggiano cheese

1 teaspoon fresh rosemary leaves, chopped

1 teaspoon kosher salt

¼ teaspoon ground black pepper

2 pounds chicken wings, separated into drumettes and flats

SAUCE:

2 tablespoons honey

1 tablespoon Dijon mustard

1 tablespoon chopped bird's-eye chili pepper

3 tablespoons crumbled blue cheese (optional)

Lettuce leaves, for garnish (optional)

1. Preheat the oven to 425°F using the convection setting. Line a sheet pan with parchment paper, then fit the pan with a wire rack.

2. In a large bowl, mix together the breadcrumbs, Parmigiano, rosemary, salt, and pepper. Toss in the wings, coating them evenly in the mixture to give them a light crust.

3. Place the wings on the wire rack and set the pan in the oven. Bake for 21 to 24 minutes, or until the wings are golden and crispy. When done, remove and plate.

4. When the wings are almost done, make the sauce: In a small saucepan, mix the honey, mustard, and chili pepper and bring to a gentle simmer over medium heat. Add the blue cheese, if using, and stir twice.

5. Drizzle the sauce over the wings while still hot and serve. Garnish the plates with fresh lettuce leaves, if desired. Store any leftover wings in the fridge for up to 4 days, and serve warm with any leftover sauce.

Using the convection setting on your oven produces the crispiest wings. If your oven doesn't have a convection setting, preheat it to 450°F.

GREEN COCONUT CURRY MUSSELS

YIELD: 2 SERVINGS · PREP TIME: 10 MINUTES, PLUS 20 MINUTES TO SOAK MUSSELS
COOK TIME: 7 MINUTES

If you're looking to spice things up on a first date, this is the dish to cook. It's exotic and a conversation piece. Just include some fresh crostini for soaking up the sauce, and your date will be asking for seconds—and a second date.

3 cloves garlic, sliced

1 tablespoon chopped fresh ginger

¼ cup fresh cilantro leaves, plus extra leaves for garnish

2 tablespoons green curry paste

1 tablespoon unsalted butter

2 pounds mussels, cleaned

½ cup dry white wine

½ cup coconut cream

½ teaspoon kosher salt

⅛ teaspoon ground black pepper

Several slices rustic sourdough bread, grilled or toasted, for serving

1. In a small or mini food processor, pulse the garlic, ginger, cilantro, and curry paste until smooth.

2. Melt the butter in a large pot over medium heat, then fry the curry mixture for 2 minutes, until lightly toasted and aromatic.

3. Add the mussels to the pot and deglaze with the wine. Turn the heat to high, cover, and cook for 2 minutes. Add the coconut cream and season with the salt and pepper. Return the lid to the pot and rapidly simmer for another 2 minutes. Discard any mussels that didn't open during cooking.

4. Garnish with some cilantro leaves and serve right from the pot with grilled or toasted bread (aka crostini).

LOVE TALK To clean mussels before cooking them, first soak them in cold salted water (about 2 tablespoons kosher salt to 3 cups water) for 20 minutes. Remove from the water with a slotted spoon and discard any mussels with shells that are broken or chipped or that are not firmly closed. Some mussels that are open, however, may be alive and safe to eat. To determine this, give them a tap with your finger (or tap lightly on the counter); if the shell doesn't close up, then discard the mussel. Finally, check to see if the beard remains on each mussel. It is a fibrous tuft that can be found along one side of the shell. If it's there, pull it out with the aid of a kitchen towel (or using tweezers or scissors) in the direction of the pointy tip end of the shell.

MORNING
GLORY

Dishes to start your day off right

VANILLA
COFFEE SYRUP

YIELD: 2 CUPS · PREP TIME: 5 MINUTES

For us, the day doesn't really start before a good cup of coffee. If coffee is a part of
your morning routine as well, make it more special with a delicious vanilla syrup.
Sit the jar by your coffee maker at home, and after every cup, your lover will
realize that nothing compares to this syrup—or the person who makes it.

2 vanilla beans (about 6 inches
long)

3 cinnamon sticks

1 teaspoon kosher salt

2 cups maple syrup

SPECIAL EQUIPMENT:

18-ounce pump-action dispenser
(optional)

1. Split the vanilla beans lengthwise and scrape the seeds into
the pump-action dispenser or an 18-ounce jar. Bend the
pods and drop them in, along with the cinnamon sticks and
salt.

2. Top with the maple syrup, then seal the jar and give it a
quick shake. Allow to sit for 30 minutes before using.

3. The syrup will keep for up to 6 months in the fridge or up to
3 weeks on the counter.

HOMEMADE GRANOLA
with YOGURT, MINT, *and* BLACK PEPPER

YIELD: 2 SERVINGS · PREP TIME: 10 MINUTES · COOK TIME: 25 MINUTES

Waking up on the right side of the bed doesn't mean much if you don't follow it with a good breakfast. Show your partner some love by making homemade granola! A black pepper and fresh mint garnish brings unexpected elegance to this simple classic that we just adore. Every time Randy makes it, it takes us back to when we first started dating.

GRANOLA:
(MAKES 9 CUPS, OR ABOUT
12 SERVINGS)

4 cups rolled oats

1 cup unsweetened shredded coconut

1 cup raw almonds

1 cup cashews

½ cup raw sunflower seeds

⅓ cup flax seeds

⅓ cup pumpkin seeds

⅓ cup unsalted butter

⅓ cup light brown sugar

⅓ cup maple syrup

½ teaspoon kosher salt

¾ teaspoon baking soda

1½ teaspoons vanilla extract

FOR TWO SERVINGS:

1½ cups Greek yogurt

1½ cups granola (from above)

1 cup fresh berries (blueberries, blackberries, raspberries, and/or strawberries)

1 tablespoon maple syrup

12 small fresh mint leaf clusters

¼ teaspoon ground black pepper

1. Preheat the oven to 325°F and line a sheet pan with parchment paper.

2. Put the oats, coconut, almonds, cashews, sunflower seeds, flax seeds, and pumpkin seeds in a large bowl and stir to combine.

3. Put the butter, brown sugar, maple syrup, and salt in a medium saucepan over medium heat. Stir to combine and continue stirring until the sugar has dissolved.

4. Bring the mixture to a boil, then remove from the heat and stir in the baking soda and vanilla (the baking soda helps with crispness and browning).

5. Pour the syrup mixture over the dry oat mixture and mix well until everything is evenly coated.

6. Transfer the mixture to the prepared pan and spread into an even layer. Bake for 8 minutes. Remove from the oven and toss the mixture, then gently press down on it with a rubber spatula and flatten it back into the pan. Bake for another 8 to 12 minutes, until golden brown.

7. Remove the pan from the oven and use the back of the rubber spatula to press the hot granola firmly down into the pan. Allow to cool completely before stirring or breaking it up. This will result in more of those prized granola clusters.

8. To serve, divide the yogurt between two bowls. Top each with ¾ cup of the granola and ½ cup of the berries. Garnish evenly with the maple syrup, mint, and black pepper.

This recipe makes more granola than you will need for two servings of yogurt, but it will keep in an airtight container in the pantry for up to 3 months. For the mint, small clusters of tender young leaves are ideal; otherwise, small leaves are fine.

When poaching eggs, crack each one into a small ramekin or bowl so that you can gently slide them into the simmering water. Before saucing the poached eggs, let them dry off by placing them under a towel for 20 seconds. This allows the sauce to hug the eggs rather than slide right off them.

EGGS BENEDICT

YIELD: 2 SERVINGS · PREP TIME: 8 MINUTES · COOK TIME: 40 MINUTES

Every great day starts with eggs benny, and if you master the art of making your hollandaise sauce from scratch, it'll become your partner's favorite meal. It's just that good!

1¼ pounds peameal bacon roast, or 6 slices Canadian bacon

1½ teaspoons extra-virgin olive oil

½ teaspoon ground black pepper

HOLLANDAISE SAUCE:

1 cup (2 sticks) unsalted butter

3 large egg yolks

1 teaspoon fresh lemon juice

1 teaspoon grainy Dijon mustard

½ teaspoon Worcestershire sauce

½ teaspoon mild hot sauce, such as Frank's

1 teaspoon kosher salt

1 teaspoon ground black pepper

4 large eggs

1 teaspoon distilled white vinegar, for the poaching water

2 English muffins, split and toasted

Snipped fresh chives, for garnish (optional)

We always use peameal here because it's so much juicier, has a better texture, and gives the dish a next-level presentation. Randy prefers a thick cut, while Katherine likes thinner slices, as shown. There will be leftovers.

1. If using Canadian bacon, skip ahead to Step 2. To prepare the peameal bacon, preheat the oven to 450°F. Rub the roast with the olive oil and pepper and place in a medium cast-iron frying pan. Roast until the internal temperature reaches 140°F, 20 to 25 minutes. Let rest for 10 minutes before carving two 1-inch slices; reserve the rest for another use.

2. Make the hollandaise: Begin by clarifying the butter in a small saucepan over medium heat until the milk solids rise to the top. It should be bubbling and foamy on top. Skim the foam from the top until the butter is clarified and transparent. Remove from the heat and let rest for 2 minutes. Residue from the milk solids will be visible at the bottom of the pan; take care to leave it behind when pouring the clarified butter.

3. Whisk the egg yolks in a bowl over a simmering water bath until they reach a frothy ribbon stage. To avoid cooking the yolks, do this intermittently: whisk for 1 minute at a time, then momentarily move the bowl off the bath. Add the lemon juice halfway through the process. Once at ribbon stage, slowly whisk the clarified butter into the yolks, then whisk in the mustard, Worcestershire, hot sauce, salt, and pepper. Slide the pan off the heat and let rest for 5 minutes.

4. If using Canadian bacon, brown the slices in a preheated frying pan over medium heat, then set aside.

5. Poach the eggs: Fill a medium saucepan with water and bring to a gentle simmer over medium heat. Add the vinegar. Swirl the water and gently slide in the eggs. Poach until they reach the desired doneness (1½ to 2 minutes for set whites with runny yolks). Lower the heat as needed to maintain a gentle simmer.

6. To serve, place an English muffin on each of two serving plates. Top with the peameal bacon or Canadian bacon, poached eggs, and hollandaise. Garnish with chives, if desired.

EGGS
with SOLDIERS

YIELD: 1 SERVING · PREP TIME: 3 MINUTES · COOK TIME: 7½ MINUTES

There's nothing more nostalgic than dipping toast into soft-boiled eggs, and this is the grown-up version, with a fresh chive and flaky sea salt garnish. It gives you an excuse to play with your food and is guaranteed to put a smile on your partner's face in the morning. Taking just 7½ minutes to prepare, this is maybe the easiest relationship hack out there. Serve in bed for bonus points.

2 large eggs

2 slices bread of choice

Unsalted butter, for the toast

FOR GARNISH:

1 tablespoon chopped fresh chives

1 teaspoon flaky sea salt

1 teaspoon ground black pepper

SPECIAL EQUIPMENT:

2 egg cups

1. Fill a small saucepan with water and bring to a boil. Gently lower the eggs into the boiling water and set a timer for 7½ minutes. Set up an ice bath to have at the ready. When the timer goes off, immediately remove the eggs from the water and submerge them in the ice bath for 1 minute.

2. While the eggs are cooking, toast the bread and smear it with butter. Cut off the crust, then cut the toast into strips about ½ inch wide. These are your soldiers.

3. Remove the eggs from the ice bath and set in the egg cups. Using a paring knife, cut off the tops of the eggs and garnish with just a touch of the chives, salt, and pepper. Serve with the soldiers and the rest of the garnishes. Supply a small spoon for adding additional garnish to each perfect bite.

Any flaky salt will be a suitable garnish for soft-boiled eggs (like Maldon or fleur de sel), but for a more dramatic effect and a slightly smoky flavor, we like to use black lava salt here.

CRISPY FETA EGG

YIELD: 1 SERVING · PREP TIME: 4 MINUTES · COOK TIME: 6 MINUTES

TikTok made us want this dish, and the app did not disappoint. These eggs have become a morning staple in our household, and we've perfected them by adding lamb. Let's just say, nothing makes Katherine have a good morning like this tasty breakfast.

3 ounces ground lamb

1 (½-inch-thick) slice baguette, cut on an angle

¼ teaspoon kosher salt

⅛ teaspoon ground black pepper

2 ounces feta cheese, crumbled

1 large egg

1½ teaspoons chili crisp or your favorite hot sauce

1. Preheat a medium cast-iron frying pan over medium-high heat. Press the ground lamb onto the cut surface of the baguette slice, pressing it evenly across to create a thin layer. Season with the salt and pepper.

2. Place the baguette slice lamb side down in the hot pan and sear until the meat is browned and cooked through, 4 to 6 minutes. Then flip it over and crisp up the other side. While the lamb is cooking, caramelize the feta.

3. Set a medium nonstick frying pan over medium-low heat. Sprinkle the feta into the pan, creating a 4-inch circle with a little well in the middle for the egg. Let the cheese cook for a couple of minutes, until it starts to caramelize for maximum crispiness, before you add the egg.

4. Crack the egg into the well in the middle of the molten feta and cover the pan with a lid. Cook for 1½ to 2 minutes for a sunny-side-up egg with a just-set white and a runny yolk. Remove to a plate and serve with the lamb-crusted baguette. Top with the chili crisp and serve.

Chili crisp, aka chili crunch, is a popular highly flavorful infused chili–oil condiment. Our favorite brand is Momofuku, but there are many other options. Once you try it, you will want to put it on everything.

KATHERINE'S PERFECT LOX BAGEL

YIELD: 1 SERVING · PREP TIME: 8 MINUTES (NOT INCLUDING TIME TO MAKE COLD-SMOKED SALMON)

After sampling lox bagels in many places, Katherine has come to the conclusion that preparing your own fresh toppings, like crispy cucumber and paper-thin red onion, and curing your own lox is always the answer. So Randy does just that and has mastered Katherine's morning bagel order. Nothing puts a smile on Katherine's face in the morning like having this bagel in hand.

1 bagel of choice, halved

3 ounces cream cheese

1 tablespoon capers

6 thin slices cucumber

3 ounces thinly sliced cold-smoked salmon (see sidebar)

8 to 10 paper-thin slices red onion

6 small pieces fresh dill fronds

1 teaspoon fresh lemon juice

1 tablespoon extra-virgin olive oil, for drizzling

⅛ teaspoon ground black pepper

Toast the bagel, if desired. Top it with all the fixings: cream cheese, capers, cucumber, smoked salmon, red onion, dill, lemon juice, olive oil, and black pepper.

Make your smoked salmon at home rather than buying it at the store. Your breakfast will be 100 percent tastier.

HOMEMADE COLD-SMOKED SALMON

YIELD: 1½ TO 2 POUNDS
PREP TIME: 5 MINUTES, PLUS 1½ HOURS TO SALT
SMOKE TIME: 2½ HOURS

1 (2½-pound) side of salmon

3 cups iodized salt

4 cups wood chips, divided

1 large bag of ice

SPECIAL EQUIPMENT:

Insulated grill (BBQ)

Wood chips

Kitchen torch

1. Check the salmon for pin bones and remove any you find. Then pat the salmon dry and cover on all sides with the salt, packing the salt well onto the surface of the fish. Place the salmon (unwrapped) in the refrigerator for 1½ hours.

2. Rinse the salmon and place on a wire rack, then set the rack over a sheet pan of ice.

3. Place the sheet pan with the salmon on the grill. Put 1 cup of the wood chips in a small cast-iron frying pan or steel smoking box and set to the side of the salmon. Get the wood chips smoking with a blowtorch, then close the grill lid. (*Note:* You're only using the grill to trap the smoke and use it as a smoker. All the heat will come from the smoking wood chips, not the grill itself.) Check the wood chips every 30 minutes to make sure they're still burning and creating smoke, and replace the ice as needed when it melts. Once the chips are burnt through, replace and repeat for a total smoke time of about 2½ hours. When it's time to remove the salmon, the ice will almost be melted and the salmon will be cold to the touch.

4. Thinly slice the salmon with a carving or boning knife, cutting off just the portion you intend to use. Unused salmon can be frozen or stored covered in the fridge for up to a week.

HAM *and* BRIE
CROISSANT PUDDING

YIELD: 2 SERVINGS · PREP TIME: 6 MINUTES · COOK TIME: 18 MINUTES

It's hard to believe that there could be such a thing as leftover croissants, but when it does happen, it's always for the best. It would be a cardinal sin not to bring them back to life in this dish. Think of it as a savory bread pudding (aka strata), but made with croissants. Talk about starting the morning off right!

2 day-old or stale croissants, sliced ¼ inch thick

1 (8-inch) wheel Brie cheese, cut into ¼-inch-thick slices

8 slices Black Forest ham

1 teaspoon fresh thyme leaves

3 large eggs

2 tablespoons milk

½ teaspoon kosher salt

⅛ teaspoon ground black pepper

1. Preheat the oven to 425°F. Line an 8-inch tart pan or cake pan with parchment paper, allowing the paper to come up the sides.

2. Assemble the pudding: Arrange the slices of croissant, Brie, and ham in the pan, standing the croissant and Brie slices upright and folding the ham slices as needed, alternating them as follows: croissant, Brie, croissant, ham, croissant, Brie, and so on. Sprinkle the thyme leaves across the surface.

3. Whisk the eggs with the milk, salt, and pepper until combined. Pour the mixture into the pan over the croissant, Brie, and ham slices. Allow the croissants to slowly absorb the mixture for 8 to 10 minutes.

4. Bake for 18 minutes, or until golden. Remove from the oven and let rest in the pan for 6 minutes before serving. Slice and enjoy.

LEEK *and* ASPARAGUS QUICHE

YIELD: 6 TO 8 SERVINGS · PREP TIME: 15 MINUTES, PLUS 30 MINUTES TO REST DOUGH
COOK TIME: 55 MINUTES

Is there anything better than starting the day with a delicious quiche? We don't think so! This version is a showstopper because we use a deeper-than-usual pan to fill it up with delicious ingredients. Plus, you can change up the vegetables according to the season, which will have you quiche-ing the cook in winter, spring, summer, and fall.

CRUST:

2¼ cups all-purpose flour

¾ cup (1½ sticks) very cold unsalted butter, cubed

6 tablespoons ice-cold water

1 teaspoon kosher salt

FILLING:

12 large eggs

1 cup heavy cream

½ cup 2% milk

2 teaspoons kosher salt, divided

1 medium leek

1 pound medium-thick asparagus

1 tablespoon unsalted butter

2 cups shredded sharp white cheddar cheese

½ cup torn fresh dill fronds

¾ cup mascarpone

½ teaspoon ground black pepper

SPECIAL EQUIPMENT:

9-inch springform pan
(3 inches deep)

1. Make the dough: Put all the ingredients for the crust in a food processor and pulse to a confetti-like texture. Dump the mixture onto the counter and work it until it comes together into a dough. Form into a disk shape, then slap it twice and wrap in plastic wrap. Chill the dough for 30 minutes.

2. Meanwhile, prepare the egg mixture and vegetables for the filling: For ultimate smoothness, pass the eggs through a fine-mesh strainer into a large bowl, using a whisk to work the eggs through the strainer. Stir in the cream and milk and season with 1 teaspoon of the salt.

3. Cut off the dark green part and the root end of the leek. Cut the leek in half lengthwise, rinse thoroughly, pat dry, and then thinly slice. Trim the tough ends off the asparagus and discard. Cut the tender tips into 2- to 3-inch lengths, then slice the rest of the asparagus spears into ¼-inch pieces.

4. In a medium frying pan over medium heat, sauté the leek in the butter just until soft, about 8 minutes, then scrape into a bowl, season with the remaining 1 teaspoon of salt, and set aside.

5. When the dough is ready to be removed from the refrigerator, preheat the oven to 375°F and generously butter the springform pan.

6. Roll out the dough between two sheets of parchment paper into a 15-inch circle. Place in the greased pan, pressing the dough into the corners and up the sides. Trim the excess.

7. Place the leek, asparagus, cheddar, and dill in the dough-lined pan and toss to distribute evenly, then spread out across the bottom of the pan. Pour the egg mixture over the top and garnish with spoonfuls of mascarpone and the pepper.

8. Bake for 45 minutes, or until the crust and filling are golden brown. For a tender quiche, be sure to remove it from the oven when there is still a slight jiggle in the center.

9. Let rest for 30 minutes before removing the sides of the pan and slicing the quiche. Serve warm or at room temperature.

Pushing the eggs through a strainer is a little extra work, but the silky finish is a more than sufficient payoff. Go heavy on the butter when greasing the pan, too. This will ensure that the crust doesn't stick.

NUTELLA
FRENCH TOAST

YIELD: 2 SERVINGS · PREP TIME: 6 MINUTES (NOT INCLUDING TIME TO COOK BACON)
COOK TIME: 10 MINUTES

There's nothing more nostalgic than Nutella and French toast, so why not combine them? We both grew up enjoying French toast and Nutella with our families, and every time we have this mash-up, we feel like kids all over again. Try indulging your partner with this fan favorite!

4 large eggs

¼ cup milk

½ teaspoon vanilla extract

1 teaspoon ground cinnamon

6 slices brioche

1 tablespoon unsalted butter

3 tablespoons hazelnut cocoa spread, such as Nutella

¼ cup maple syrup

1 banana, sliced

4 strips bacon, cooked until crispy

½ teaspoon flaky sea salt

½ teaspoon powdered sugar

SPECIAL EQUIPMENT:

3-inch ring mold

1. In a medium bowl, whisk together the eggs, milk, vanilla, and cinnamon.

2. Punch the brioche slices with the ring mold to make perfect circles. Then soak the brioche circles in the egg batter for 2 minutes.

3. Melt the butter in a large nonstick frying pan over medium heat. When melted, add the egg-coated slices of brioche, three at a time, and fry until golden brown on both sides, about 5 minutes total.

4. Spread the top of each piece of French toast with Nutella, using about 1½ teaspoons per piece.

5. Stack the French toast pieces on two plates, three per plate, and garnish with the maple syrup, banana slices, and crispy bacon. Finish the whole thing off with the flaky salt and powdered sugar.

Using brioche or any egg-rich bread (like challah) is a game changer because the eggs in the bread make the French toast sweeter and more decadent. But you can make this recipe using any bread you have on hand, even bagels. Just remember, the denser or heavier the bread, the longer it should soak in the egg batter.

OSCAR'S SMOKED SALMON *and* POTATO ROSTI

YIELD: 4 SERVINGS · PREP TIME: 10 MINUTES · COOK TIME: 14 MINUTES

Back in the day, Randy owned a little restaurant called Oscar's, and Katherine worked there. So when Randy started to sell a prepared form of this dish from the restaurant in boutique grocery stores, it was Katherine's job to travel all over Ontario offering samples to customers. It quickly became one of our favorite dishes in the entire world, and it's kind of responsible for our relationship. So, in our opinion, it's the best way we can start the day, because we fall in love all over again every time we eat it.

2 or 3 Yukon Gold potatoes (about 18 ounces total), peeled and shredded

¼ cup clarified butter, melted

1 teaspoon kosher salt

1 teaspoon ground black pepper

FOR GARNISH:

3 ounces Maple Syrup Smoked Salmon (page 114)

¼ cup crème fraîche

1 tablespoon maple syrup

½ teaspoon ground black pepper

1. Submerge the shredded potatoes in water and give them an aggressive stir to wash off the starch.

2. Drain the potatoes, then place in a clean kitchen towel and squeeze all the liquid out. Like *really* squeeze—moisture is the enemy. To get every bit of moisture out, spread the potatoes on a paper towel and press the potatoes onto the paper towel.

3. Dump the potatoes into a bowl, then toss with the melted butter and season with the salt and pepper.

4. Lightly preheat a 10-inch nonstick frying pan over medium heat. Put the potato mixture in the pan, spread it into an even layer, and tuck in the edges, then turn the heat down to medium-low. Cook until the edges start to crisp up and become golden, 6 to 7 minutes, then give the beauty a flip and continue to cook for another 6 to 7 minutes, until golden on the outside and creamy on the inside.

5. Remove and cut into four wedges. Garnish with the smoked salmon along with its herbed glaze topping, crème fraîche, maple syrup, and pepper.

The key steps in making rosti are rinsing off the potato starch and getting the shredded potatoes really dry before tossing them with the clarified butter. If you can't pull off the flip, simply put a plate over your pan and turn it upside down. Now slide the rosti back into the pan to crisp up the other side.

QUICKIES

Recipes in 20 minutes or less for date night or any occasion

CRAB CAKES

YIELD: 4 CRAB CAKES (1 PER SERVING)
PREP TIME: 12 MINUTES, PLUS 10 MINUTES TO CHILL · COOK TIME: 8 MINUTES

Katherine's love language is crab. So, whenever Randy wants to spoil her or score a few brownie points, these crab cakes are the way to go. They look impressive, taste delicious, and will knock the socks off the special someone you're looking to impress, or at least secure that next date.

CRAB CAKES:

1 pound lump crab meat

1 large egg

3 tablespoons mayonnaise

1 tablespoon Dijon mustard

1 teaspoon Worcestershire sauce

Juice of 1 lemon

1 cup plain breadcrumbs

1 handful fresh parsley, chopped

1 teaspoon kosher salt

1 teaspoon ground black pepper

1 tablespoon extra-virgin olive oil, for the pan

1 tablespoon unsalted butter, for the pan

MUSTARD SAUCE:

1 cup mayonnaise

2 tablespoons heavy cream

1 tablespoon dry mustard

2 teaspoons Worcestershire sauce

1 teaspoon A.1. Sauce

Grated zest and juice of ½ lemon

1 teaspoon kosher salt

FOR GARNISH:

1 cup very thinly sliced fennel

1 teaspoon thinly sliced pencil chilies or bird's-eye chilies

1 teaspoon very thinly sliced fresh chives

1. Make the crab cakes: Put all the ingredients, except the olive oil and butter, in a mixing bowl and, using your hands, gently mix together, keeping some of the larger crab lumps intact.

2. Divide the crab mixture into four equal portions, about 5 ounces each, and form each into a large cake about 1½ inches thick. Place the crab cakes on a plate and set in the refrigerator to chill for 5 to 10 minutes.

3. Preheat the oven to 375°F.

4. Heat the olive oil and butter in a large cast-iron frying pan or other oven-safe pan over medium heat. Gently lay the crab cakes in the hot pan, working in two batches if needed to avoid crowding. Cook until golden on the underside, 3 to 4 minutes, then carefully flip. If frying in batches, remove the partially cooked crab cakes to a plate and repeat with the remaining crab cakes.

5. Place the pan with the partially cooked crab cakes golden side up in the oven. Bake for 7 minutes, or until golden on all sides.

6. While the crab cakes are in the oven, make the mustard sauce: Combine all the ingredients in a medium bowl and set aside.

7. Serve the crab cakes with the sauce and garnish with the fennel, chilies, and chives.

You need to be very gentle when working this crab cake mixture. You spent a lot of money on those crab lumps, so keep them lumpy for the best results.

GAMBAS *al* AJILO (SPANISH-STYLE GARLIC SHRIMP)

YIELD: 3 TO 4 SERVINGS · PREP TIME: 3 MINUTES · COOK TIME: 8 MINUTES

Spain is our culinary mecca and our go-to destination whenever we travel. This dish transports us there in under 10 minutes. So, if you're looking to take that special someone in your life on a culinary adventure, this spicy shrimp has you covered—no passports required. And you only have to dirty one pan!

1 pound colossal black tiger shrimp (aka prawns) (6 to 8 ct), peeled and deveined

1 teaspoon kosher salt

1 teaspoon ground black pepper

2 tablespoons unsalted butter

2 tablespoons extra-virgin olive oil

5 cloves garlic, sliced

2 pencil chilies or cherry bomb chilies, sliced

1 big handful fresh flat-leaf parsley, chopped

Juice of 1 lemon

1 loaf crusty bread, for serving

1. Season the shrimp with the salt and pepper.

2. In a sauté pan over medium-low heat, melt the butter in the oil. Then lightly toast the garlic and chilies, 1 to 2 minutes.

3. Add the seasoned shrimp to the pan and gently fry on both sides just until they are firm and opaque, about 2 minutes per side.

4. Sprinkle with the parsley and finish with the lemon juice. Adjust the seasoning if needed.

5. Serve with crusty bread.

Tiger shrimp sometimes come packaged with the heads and tails on. You don't need them for this recipe, but don't throw them out; use them to make homemade shellfish stock. Also, don't be a shrimp and overcook them.

KULAJDA (CZECH-STYLE MUSHROOM SOUP)

YIELD: 4 SERVINGS · PREP TIME: 10 MINUTES · COOK TIME: 20 MINUTES

This is one of the first dishes that Katherine ever made for Randy. She spent a lot of time in the Czech Republic, and this soup became an instant favorite. It's a little peculiar, so it had Randy scratching his head when he first tasted it. But it's creamy, sour, complex, and delicious—a great way to impress a special someone and keep them guessing.

2 cups mixed mushrooms (such as porcini, enoki, and/or cremini), roughly chopped

2 tablespoons unsalted butter, divided

2 tablespoons all-purpose flour

2 tablespoons white wine vinegar

1 tablespoon honey

3 cups chicken stock

1 pound yellow potatoes, peeled and cubed

¾ cup heavy cream

½ teaspoon kosher salt

½ teaspoon ground black pepper

4 large eggs

1 teaspoon distilled white vinegar, for the poaching water

3 tablespoons roughly chopped fresh dill, for garnish

1. In a medium frying pan over medium heat, sauté the mushrooms in 1 tablespoon of the butter until softened, about 4 minutes. Season lightly with salt and set aside.

2. Make a roux: Melt the remaining 1 tablespoon of butter in a soup pot over medium heat. Add the flour and cook, stirring constantly, for 2 minutes, or until blonde. It will create a bubbling mass.

3. Add the vinegar and honey to the pot, then gradually pour in the chicken stock while stirring to prevent lumps. Taste and adjust the seasoning to your liking, then bring to a boil.

4. Add the potatoes and reduce the heat to low. Cover with a lid and cook for 10 minutes, or until tender.

5. While the potatoes are boiling, poach the eggs: Fill a medium saucepan with water and bring to a gentle simmer over medium heat. Add the vinegar. Swirl the water and gently slide in the eggs. Poach until they reach the desired doneness (1½ to 2 minutes for set whites with runny yolks).

6. When the potatoes are tender, remove the pot from the heat and stir in the cream, salt, and pepper. Let the soup sit for 5 minutes.

7. Serve in shallow soup bowls with the sautéed mushrooms and a poached egg, garnished with the fresh dill.

Like dating, you need to put in the work with this recipe. Having your mise en place ready to go is the make-or-break of this dish, because if your soup is ready but the other ingredients are not, it'll be botched and you'll have to start all over again. Who wants that?

MUFFULETTA

YIELD: 2 SANDWICHES (1 PER SERVING) · PREP TIME: 5 MINUTES · COOK TIME: 8 MINUTES

A muffuletta is one sandwich that Randy could eat for every foreseeable date night. We tried one on our first trip to New Orleans together, where we stumbled into Napoleon House and split a muffuletta. We were instantly smitten. Since it's hard to find a great muffuletta outside the Big Easy, we had to recreate it for you and your date to share at home.

1 tablespoon unsalted butter

1 clove garlic, cut in half

2 sesame seed hamburger buns, split

8 slices mortadella

12 slices Genoa salami

8 slices deli ham

4 slices provolone cheese

4 slices Swiss cheese

OLIVE SALAD:

½ cup green olives, chopped

¼ cup roasted red peppers, chopped

1 handful fresh basil, chopped

1 tablespoon extra-virgin olive oil

Juice of 1 large lemon wedge

½ teaspoon kosher salt

½ teaspoon ground black pepper

1. Make the olive salad: Mix together the olives, peppers, and basil in a bowl. Season with the olive oil, lemon juice, salt, and pepper.

2. Set a 10-inch cast-iron frying pan over medium heat and allow to heat up. Melt the butter in a second 10-inch cast-iron frying pan over medium-high heat and add the garlic. Toast the buns cut side down in the garlic butter, then remove from the pan and evenly layer the meats and cheeses on the bottom buns.

3. Top the sandwiches with the olive salad and then the top halves of the buns. Set the sandwiches in the frying pan and place over medium-low heat. Press down with the second preheated frying pan until the sandwiches are warm and crispy and the cheese is soft and melty.

4. Cut each sandwich into quarters and serve.

The secret to a successful muffuletta comes down to the press. It brings it all together; without it, the sandwich would fall apart. Just like a relationship, you must press forward to stick together.

RAPINI LINGUINE
with BURRATA

YIELD: 4 SERVINGS · PREP TIME: 5 MINUTES · COOK TIME: 15 MINUTES

We consider rapini to be *the* cruciferous green in our household. It's beautiful, bright, and blends perfectly with the strands of linguine and creamy burrata in this pasta dish. Plus, pasta is the way to almost anyone's heart. Once you whip up this recipe, they'll fall for you quicker than you can refill their bowl.

4 shallots, sliced

4 cloves garlic, sliced

½ pepperoncini, sliced

2 tablespoons extra-virgin olive oil, plus extra for garnish

1 cup dry white wine

½ cup vegetable stock

Grated zest and juice of 1 lemon

1 bunch rapini, chopped

1 teaspoon kosher salt

1 teaspoon ground black pepper

2 tablespoons cashews

1 handful fresh basil

1 pound linguine

1 cup grated Parmigiano-Reggiano cheese

2 (4-ounce) balls burrata

1. In a large frying pan over medium heat, sauté the shallots, garlic, and pepperoncini in the olive oil.

2. Deglaze the pan with the wine, stock, and lemon juice, then stir in the rapini and season with the salt and pepper. Cover with a lid and simmer for 4 minutes, or until fork-tender.

3. Remove the pan from the heat and carefully transfer the rapini mixture to a blender or food processor. Add the lemon zest, cashews, and basil and blend until smooth. Return the mixture to the pan and set aside.

4. Bring a large pot of salted water to a boil. Add the pasta and cook until it's not quite al dente (it should be about 70 percent done). Reserve about 1 cup of the cooking water, then drain the pasta.

5. Add the pasta to the sauce and toss to coat, adding a little of the pasta water as needed to finish cooking the pasta and achieve a creamy consistency. Toss in the Parmigiano-Reggiano.

6. Top each serving with half a burrata ball and garnish with olive oil, salt, and black pepper.

Cooking the pasta to about 70 percent done in the water and finishing it off in the sauce, until al dente, makes for the best-tasting pasta since the flavor of the sauce infuses the pasta as it finishes cooking.

LAMB MEATBALLS
with MINT TZATZIKI

YIELD: 4 SERVINGS (AS AN APPETIZER) · PREP TIME: 12 MINUTES · COOK TIME: 12 MINUTES

If you and your date love the unique flavor of lamb as much as Katherine does, then this dish is about to become the holy grail in your relationship. It's the perfect appetizer to kick off date night and share how your day was. Be warned: You may fight over the last meatball because they are just that good!

TZATZIKI:

½ cup seeded and shredded cucumber

2 cups full-fat Greek yogurt

Grated zest and juice of 1 lemon

½ clove garlic, grated

1 tablespoon chopped fresh dill

2 teaspoons ground black pepper

1 teaspoon kosher salt

1 handful fresh mint leaves, for garnish

LAMB MEATBALLS:

1 pound ground lamb

1 clove garlic, grated

¼ medium yellow onion, grated

¼ cup grated Manchego cheese

2 tablespoons full-fat Greek yogurt

1 teaspoon harissa

1½ teaspoons kosher salt

1 teaspoon ground black pepper

1 teaspoon dried oregano leaves

1 quart lamb or beef stock, for poaching

FOR GARNISH:

1 tablespoon extra-virgin olive oil

2 tablespoons chopped roasted and salted pistachios

1 tablespoon chopped fresh dill

1. Make the tzatziki: Salt and drain the cucumber, then squeeze out the excess water. Combine all the ingredients for the tzatziki in a medium bowl and set aside.

2. Make the meatballs: Using your hands, mix together all the ingredients except the stock, then roll into balls about 1¼ inches in diameter (you should get about 16 meatballs). Place on a plate and let rest in the fridge for 5 minutes.

3. In a sauté pan, bring the stock to a gentle simmer over medium heat. (It should be about 1½ inches deep; add more stock or water as needed to achieve that depth.) Poach the meatballs in the stock, adjusting the heat as needed to keep the stock at a bare simmer, until they reach an internal temperature of 145°F, 6 to 9 minutes.

4. Transfer the meatballs to a medium frying pan and add about ½ cup of the poaching liquid. Cook over medium heat, swirling the pan from time to time, until the liquid has almost completely evaporated and the meatballs are glazed, 4 to 5 minutes.

5. To serve, spread some tzatziki on a plate, then drizzle with the olive oil. Top with the meatballs and garnish with the pistachios and dill.

Always poach your meatballs to keep them moist. You don't want them or your relationship to dry out. You can also use the leftover poaching liquid as the base for a soup, pho, or beef stew.

BLUE CHEESE MUSHROOM TOAST

YIELD: 2 TOASTS (1 PER SERVING) · PREP TIME: 6 MINUTES · COOK TIME: 4 MINUTES

We're always looking for fun new ways to enjoy blue cheese, and this fancy snack
does not disappoint. It comes together so quickly, and we devour it just as fast.
Not to be mushy, but this dish will definitely raise a toast on your next date night.

1 tablespoon unsalted butter

3 cloves garlic, thinly sliced

2 slices sourdough bread

3 cups mixed wild mushrooms, torn and/or sliced

1 teaspoon kosher salt

½ teaspoon ground black pepper

½ cup crumbled blue cheese

1. Melt the butter in a sauté pan over medium heat. Add the garlic and fry in the butter until golden brown.

2. Add the mushrooms and season with the salt and pepper. Sauté until soft and tender, about 5 minutes.

3. Toast the bread so it has a soft crunch.

4. Spread the blue cheese on the toasted bread.

5. Top with the mushrooms and serve.

If you or your date are not a fan of blue cheese, you can swap it out for fresh goat cheese or ricotta.

HEIRLOOM TOMATO SALAD

YIELD: 2 SERVINGS · PREP TIME: 3 MINUTES, PLUS TIME TO MARINATE TOMATOES

If you ask Randy, he'll say it took him forty-nine years to find the perfect tomato salad. At our favorite restaurant in San Sebastián, which we visited multiple times during our honeymoon, they made this salad with the simplest and most flavorful ingredients. So, we had to bring it home and put our own spin on it by peeling and marinating the tomatoes. It's the perfect way to start any date night.

3 medium heirloom tomatoes

2 tablespoons white wine vinegar

2 tablespoons extra-virgin olive oil

1 teaspoon flaky sea salt

1. Peel the tomatoes with a sharp paring knife and cut into wedges.

2. In a medium bowl, marinate the tomatoes in the vinegar for about 10 minutes.

3. Plate the tomato wedges one by one, leaving the excess juice in the bowl.

4. Drizzle with the olive oil and sprinkle with the flaky salt.

When it comes to peeling tomatoes, you would usually blanch and shock them beforehand. But this harms your fragile ripe tomatoes, affecting the mouthfeel and jeopardizing the quality. Instead, try peeling them raw and go heavy on the vinegar for the most flavorful results. Plus, you can use the leftover juices to make some delicious cocktails, oyster shooters, or salad dressings.

BIKINI
HAM *and* CHEESE

YIELD: 1 SERVING · PREP TIME: 2 MINUTES · COOK TIME: 3 MINUTES

Mornings call for a breakfast sandwich. So wake up your partner with the smallest, cutest friggin' sandwich. It may be simple, but just watch what happens after they take a bite.

1½ teaspoons unsalted butter, softened

2 slices white bread

1 teaspoon Dijon mustard

1 slice smoked ham

1 slice Gruyère cheese

FOR GARNISH:

1 cornichon

1 pickled onion

1. Spread the butter on the outsides of the bread slices and the mustard on the other sides. Layer the ham and cheese on the mustard sides.

2. Toast the sandwich in a medium frying pan over medium heat, pressing down with a spatula as it cooks to get it nice and thin. When the bread is golden on one side, flip and cook until it's golden on both sides and the cheese is melted, about 3 minutes total.

3. Trim off the crusts and cut the sandwich in half. Garnish with the cornichon and pickled onion and serve.

Sometimes less is more, so don't overstuff this one.

MEET THE
PARENTS

Standout recipes that'll be sure to win over
the future in-laws

ROSÉ GRILLED OYSTERS

YIELD: 4 SERVINGS · PREP TIME: 10 MINUTES · COOK TIME: 8 MINUTES

We are huge fans of oysters. We like them prepared every which way: raw (see Oyster Shooter, page 45), baked (see Oysters Rockefeller, page 49), and grilled, as prepared here. This is a great way to serve oysters when entertaining. Everyone always likes to gather around the barbecue, and it's a great starter for newbies to oysters because it takes out the rawness and adds a punch of flavor. The parents will love them.

ROSÉ-INFUSED BUTTER:

½ cup (1 stick) unsalted butter

1½ teaspoons chopped garlic

¼ cup dry rosé wine

1 tablespoon chopped fresh parsley

1 teaspoon chopped fresh tarragon

½ teaspoon Dijon mustard

½ teaspoon Worcestershire sauce

¼ teaspoon mild hot sauce, such as Frank's

1 teaspoon fresh lemon juice

1 teaspoon kosher salt

¼ teaspoon ground black pepper

12 oysters

SPECIAL EQUIPMENT:

Oyster knife

1. Make the rosé-infused butter: Melt the butter in a small saucepan over medium heat. Add the garlic and gently simmer for 3 minutes. Then pour in the rosé and whisk in the remaining ingredients. Remove the pan from the heat and let rest.

2. Preheat a grill to high heat.

3. Shuck the oysters. Create two rows of slightly mounded kosher salt on a sheet pan. (This will help keep the oyster shells in place so you don't lose precious oyster liquor or the melted butter topping as you carry them to the grill.) Place the oysters on the beds of salt and fill each oyster with the rosé butter mixture.

4. Grill for 4 to 6 minutes, or until the butter starts to simmer. You're looking to softly poach the oysters in the melted butter. Remove and enjoy.

When shucking oysters, use a bar rag or kitchen towel to securely hold the oyster in one hand. The towel will help to protect your hand. (You can wear a special glove designed to protect your hand, if you're not confident.) Then, using your other hand, get the oyster knife into the oyster and twist it open. Do not leverage and pry because it will break the shell. Reserve the oyster liquor.

This method is great because it's simple math. You can use the formula—5 minutes of roasting per pound of meat—for any size of bone-in prime rib. So the roasting time for a 5-pound prime rib is 25 minutes, 6 pounds 30 minutes, 8 pounds 40 minutes, 12 pounds 60 minutes. See the pattern? But don't underestimate the importance of the meat being at room temperature before roasting and not opening the oven door for 2 hours after roasting. Don't do it, even if you are tempted to. Give it space, like you do in your relationship.

PRIME RIB
au JUS

YIELD: 8 TO 10 SERVINGS · PREP TIME: 15 MINUTES, PLUS 2 HOURS TO TEMPER AND
2 HOURS TO REST IN OVEN · COOK TIME: 50 MINUTES

Let's just say that with this dish, Randy instantly won over Katherine's family and friends. We can't even count the number of times he's been asked to make it since. So, if you're looking to get in the good books with your partner's loved ones, this is the way. The best part is, prime rib is so easy to prepare—it's all based on following a few simple rules.

1 (10-pound) bone-in prime rib (aka standing rib roast)

½ cup Dijon mustard

8 cloves garlic, chopped

¼ cup chopped fresh rosemary

3 tablespoons kosher salt

1 tablespoon ground black pepper

¼ cup diced carrots

¼ cup diced celery

¼ cup diced onions

1 tablespoon unsalted butter

1 cup dry red wine

FOR SERVING:

2 teaspoons prepared horseradish

2 teaspoons chopped fresh chives

1. Pull the prime rib out of the fridge 2 hours before cooking to temper the meat and allow it to come to room temperature.

2. Preheat the oven to 475°F, using the convection setting. If your oven doesn't have a convection setting, preheat it to 500°F.

3. Mix together the Dijon mustard, garlic, rosemary, salt, and pepper. Pat the prime rib dry, then coat every inch of it with the mustard paste.

4. Place on a rack in a roasting pan and set on the middle rack in the oven. Roast for exactly 5 minutes per pound. For the 10-pound size called for in this recipe, the roasting time is 50 minutes. If the prime rib you purchased is smaller or larger, adjust the cooking time accordingly based on this formula.

5. Kill the heat without opening the oven door. Then set the timer for another 2 hours. Do not open the door until the 2 hours are up. This allows the meat to gently finish cooking and results in meat that is medium-rare throughout, not just in the center.

6. After 2 hours, remove the roast from the oven. Carve the back of the ribs off the roast. Deboning the roast will allow you to carve perfectly pink slices in more consistent portions.

7. Pour the pan juices into a smaller container and skim the fat from the top; set aside. Place the roasting pan on the stovetop over medium heat and sweat the vegetables in the butter. When the vegetables are soft, deglaze the pan with the wine and cook until reduced by half. Pour in the reserved pan juices, simmer for 4 minutes, and then strain.

8. Serve the roast with the pan juices, horseradish, and chives.

MAPLE SYRUP
SMOKED SALMON

YIELD: 4 TO 6 SERVINGS · PREP TIME: 12 MINUTES, PLUS 1 HOUR TO BRINE
SMOKE TIME: 30 TO 60 MINUTES

Like meeting your future in-laws, making smoked salmon can be a little intimidating, but
it doesn't have to be difficult. With the right fish, brine, and glaze, you'll not only master
this dish but also master the art of impressing your partner's parents. Just be warned:
they might like the salmon more than they like you. At least at first.

BRINE:

3 tablespoons kosher salt

¼ cup maple syrup

2 tablespoons fresh lemon juice

SALMON:

½ whole skin-on salmon fillet
(about 2½ pounds), preferably
center-cut, pin bones removed

GLAZE:

3 tablespoons maple syrup

1 tablespoon chopped fresh chives

1 tablespoon chopped fresh dill

1 tablespoon chopped fresh
parsley

1 teaspoon peppercorns, cracked

SPECIAL EQUIPMENT:
Smoker and wood chips, or grill
and wood chips with smoke box or
other wood chip smoker accessory

1. Mix together the brine ingredients in a 1-gallon zip-top bag.
   Add the salmon, seal the bag, and refrigerate for 1 hour,
   turning the salmon every 15 minutes. Remove the fish from the
   brine and pat dry.

2. Get your smoker smoking at 220°F, and line a sheet pan with
   parchment paper. (If using a grill, set it up for indirect cooking
   with low heat using a smoker accessory, such as a smoke
   box.) Then place the salmon in the lined pan and hot-smoke
   for 15 minutes.

3. Mix together the glaze ingredients and spoon or brush on the
   salmon. Continue to smoke until the internal temperature hits
   132°F, periodically basting with any excess glaze that collects
   in the pan.

4. Remove from the smoker and let rest for 15 minutes. Serve
   hot, at room temperature, or chilled.

When it comes to salmon, always buy the best and support your
local fishmonger. They know what's up. Be sure to explain that
you'll be making smoked salmon; they'll know what quality of fish
you'll need. When it comes to hot smoking, we prefer to use our
Napoleon grill, as it has a wood chip tray accessory that allows us
to use the grill as a smoker.

We can't emphasize this enough: The trick to getting a crunchy outer crust on this roast is to dry out the pork belly skin and to keep the skin dry as you're working with it. Step 1 calls for drying the pork belly for 24 hours before salting it for 8 hours, but if you can, go for an initial drying time of 48 to 72 hours before the salting step. You won't regret it! If you don't like much heat, seed the chili peppers before chopping them. New to using sumac? This is a great recipe to become acquainted. Its floral acidity perfectly balances the fatty pork belly.

SUMAC PORCHETTA

YIELD: 8 TO 14 SERVINGS · PREP TIME: 25 MINUTES, PLUS 32 HOURS TO DRY AND SALT PORK BELLY SKIN · COOK TIME: 2 HOURS

If you're going to meet the parents, you've gotta bring the meat! So why not have some fun with it and make this stuffed pork roast? Thanks to an outer layer of skin-on pork belly, it has a shatteringly crisp crust but remains incredibly moist on the inside. Not only will it fill everyone up, but they'll be able to take home leftovers and talk about it—and your impressive cooking skills—for days to come.

4 pounds pork belly, skin on

1 cup kosher salt

FILLING:

2 tablespoons ground sumac

¼ cup chopped fresh dill

3 tablespoons chopped pencil chilies or cherry bomb chilies

1 tablespoon chopped garlic

1½ teaspoons kosher salt

1½ teaspoons ground black pepper

1 pound pork tenderloin, about 2 inches in diameter

SPECIAL EQUIPMENT:

Butcher twine

Meat thermometer

1. Remove the pork belly from its packaging and place it skin side up in the refrigerator for 24 hours. Set it as close to the refrigerator fan as possible, and leave it uncovered.

2. After 24 hours, cover the skin with the salt and put the pork belly back in the fridge for 8 hours, or overnight. Yes, uncovered. You are drying out the skin.

3. The following day (or 8 hours later), remove the salt and pat the pork belly completely dry with paper towels.

4. Preheat the oven to 500°F and set a wire rack in a sheet pan.

5. Place the pork belly skin side down on a dry cutting board and season with the sumac, dill, chilies, garlic, salt, and black pepper. Lay the tenderloin right down the middle, close the pork belly around the tenderloin, and tie it shut as tightly as you can with butcher twine. Try to keep the skin as dry as possible while you're working.

6. Place the wrapped pork in the oven and roast for 35 minutes. Crackling should appear on the skin. Turn the oven temperature down to 350°F (using the convection setting) and roast for another 85 minutes, or until the temperature in the center of the roast reaches 145°F. If the skin still isn't super crispy, broil on high for a couple minutes.

7. Let rest for 20 minutes before slicing. When ready to serve, slice the porchetta in half lengthwise, then cut crosswise into portions of your desired thickness, making sure everyone gets a nice piece of crackling (the crispy goodness).

THREE-CHEESE
CHICKEN PARMIGIANA

YIELD: 4 SERVINGS · PREP TIME: 15 MINUTES · COOK TIME: 15 MINUTES

If you're looking to ease your way into meeting and impressing your partner's parents, this classic chicken dish will do the trick. Its cheesy and saucy goodness makes this the ultimate comfort food that'll have everyone feeling relaxed and at ease.

TOMATO SAUCE:

1 tablespoon chopped garlic

1 tablespoon chopped shallots

3 tablespoons extra-virgin olive oil

1 (14.5-ounce) can whole peeled tomatoes, crushed

1 teaspoon kosher salt

CHICKEN:

2 cups plain breadcrumbs

2 cups panko breadcrumbs

1 cup grated Parmigiano-Reggiano cheese

1 teaspoon kosher salt

½ teaspoon ground black pepper

3 large eggs, beaten

4 large boneless, skinless chicken breasts (8 to 10 ounces each), butterflied and pounded to ¼ inch thick

¼ cup all-purpose flour, for dusting the chicken

¼ cup extra-virgin olive oil, for the pan

CHEESE TOPPING:

1 (7-ounce) ball fresh mozzarella di bufala

1 (1-pound) block mozzarella cheese, sliced

1 cup grated Parmigiano-Reggiano cheese

2 handfuls fresh basil leaves

1. Start with the tomato sauce: In a large saucepan over medium heat, toast the garlic and shallots in the olive oil until golden. Add the tomatoes and salt and lower the heat to maintain a soft simmer. Continue to cook until reduced by one-quarter.

2. Bread the chicken: In a shallow bowl or rimmed plate, mix the two types of breadcrumbs with the Parmigiano-Reggiano. Season with the salt and pepper. Pour the beaten eggs into another shallow bowl (or rimmed plate). Dust the chicken on both sides with the flour, then dip into the egg wash and finish by pressing the chicken into the breadcrumb mixture.

3. Bring the olive oil up to temperature in a 12-inch cast-iron frying pan over medium heat. When the oil hits 300°F, gently place a breaded chicken breast in the oil, moving away from you. When the underside is golden, about 2 minutes, flip and continue cooking until both sides are golden and crispy. Repeat with the remaining three pieces of chicken, making sure the olive oil has returned to temperature before placing the chicken in the pan. Add more olive oil as needed to maintain a depth of ¼ inch in the pan.

4. Place the chicken pieces in a baking dish large enough to fit all four in a single layer. Or, if you have four individual serving plates that are oven safe, place each piece in its own oven-safe dish for serving directly from oven to table. Top with the tomato sauce, cheeses, and basil leaves. Broil on the middle rack until the cheese is completely melted and beginning to brown, about 6 minutes. Remove and serve.

Broiling the chicken Parmigiana in individual oven-safe serving dishes gives the meal a cool factor and extra-crispy bits that your future in-laws can't help but love. It's an especially appreciated touch in the wintertime. Just remind them that the plates are hot! Fresh mozzarella di bufala—mozzarella made from the milk of water buffaloes—makes this dish extra-special. If you can't find it, fresh mozzarella made from cow's milk is fine.

PISTACHIO CHIVE–CRUSTED RACK *of* LAMB *with* MINT SAUCE

YIELD: 4 SERVINGS · PREP TIME: 10 MINUTES, PLUS 13 MINUTES TO REST · COOK TIME: 20 MINUTES

If you're looking to pull out the big guns, lamb is always the answer—and especially rack of lamb. This particular preparation is so packed with flavor and so tender, with a satisfying bit of crunch on top. It's a cause for celebration. If this doesn't impress the socks off the parents, nothing will.

2 full racks of lamb (2 pounds each), frenched

2 teaspoons kosher salt

1 teaspoon ground black pepper

2 tablespoons Dijon mustard

1 cup shelled pistachios, chopped

¼ cup thinly sliced fresh chives

MINT SAUCE:
(MAKES ¾ CUP)

2 tablespoons granulated sugar

½ cup dry red wine

2 tablespoons red wine vinegar

½ cup chopped fresh mint

½ teaspoon kosher salt

¼ teaspoon ground black pepper

1. Score the fat caps on the racks of lamb and season on all sides with the salt and pepper.

2. Preheat the oven to 425°F.

3. Place a rack of lamb fat cap side down in a large cast-iron frying pan over medium heat; render the fat for about 4 minutes. Drain the fat and repeat with the second rack.

4. Place both racks fat side up in the pan, transfer the pan to the oven, and roast for 8 minutes, or until the internal temperature hits 100°F. Remove and let rest for 5 minutes, then flip the racks of lamb fat side down. Return the pan to the oven and continue roasting until the internal temperature reaches 120°F, 8 to 10 minutes. Remove and let rest for 8 minutes.

5. While the lamb is resting, make the mint sauce: In a small saucepan over medium-low heat, dissolve the sugar in the wine, then stir in the vinegar. Transfer the mixture to a serving bowl and, once completely cool, stir in the mint, salt, and pepper.

6. Paint the lamb with the mustard and crust with the pistachios and chives. Roast for 2 more minutes, just to toast the nuts. Remove and carve between the ribs. Serve with the mint sauce on the side.

Frenching the racks of lamb makes this dish look so much more sophisticated. The parents will be thinking, "This person has it together." When frenching a rack of lamb, you're removing the meat and fat from the first 2 inches of bone. It's something you can do yourself at home (there are many tutorials on YouTube), or, if you prefer, you can ask your butcher to french the racks for you.

CRISPY MACKEREL
with VIERGE SAUCE

YIELD: 4 SERVINGS ▪ PREP TIME: 8 MINUTES ▪ COOK TIME: 6 MINUTES

If you're hosting the parents for lunch or a light dinner, this is your go-to.
Pair it with a delish bottle of rosé and you'll all feel like you've been
transported to a patio in southern France. It's definitely a crowd-pleaser.

CRISPY MACKEREL:

4 skin-on mackerel fillets (about 5 ounces each), pin bones removed

½ teaspoon kosher salt

¼ teaspoon ground black pepper

VIERGE SAUCE:

¼ cup extra-virgin olive oil

2 cloves garlic, finely diced

2 Roma tomatoes, peeled, seeded, and finely diced

24 Castelvetrano olives, pitted and diced

Juice of 1 lemon

1 teaspoon kosher salt

FOR GARNISH:

1 handful fresh micro basil leaves

1. Get a charcoal grill ripping hot and bring the grates right down to just above the charcoal for maximum sear.

2. Season the mackerel fillets on both sides with the salt and set aside for a couple of minutes while the grill heats up, then pat the skin dry. Season the fillets with the pepper and place skin side down on the grill, right above the coals. Cook the mackerel until the skin is charred and crispy and the fish is 80 percent of the way done, about 2 minutes, depending on the exact thickness of your fillets. Remove and allow to finish cooking all the way through off the heat. Slice the fillets into 2-inch pieces.

3. Place a medium frying pan on the cool side of the grill and slowly heat the olive oil until it's warm but not hot. Sweat the garlic in the oil, then add the tomatoes, olives, salt, and lemon juice and bring to a gentle simmer. Remove from the heat and season with the salt.

4. Plate the sauce, then top with the crispy fish and garnish with the micro basil.

LOVE TAP Patting the skin dry before grilling will give you a nice char and a crispy finish.

SALT-BAKED SNAPPER

YIELD: 4 TO 6 SERVINGS · PREP TIME: 12 MINUTES · COOK TIME: 40 MINUTES

When it comes to making dinner for the parents of your significant other, you need a showstopper that grabs their attention. This salt-baked snapper will do just that. The presentation and flavor alone will keep you on their mind for the foreseeable future.

4 egg whites

2 pounds kosher salt

1 (2- to 2.5-pound) whole snapper, cleaned and scaled (see note)

1 lemon, sliced

1 cup fresh dill fronds

FOR SERVING:

2 lemons, cut into wedges

3 tablespoons extra-virgin olive oil

1. Preheat the oven to 425°F. Lay a piece of parchment paper cut to the size of your fish on a sheet pan.

2. Lightly whisk the egg whites, then add the salt and mix thoroughly. Lay down a thin layer of the salt mixture on the prepared pan.

3. Place the fish over the salt and stuff the cavity with the lemon slices and dill. Cover the fish with the remaining salt.

4. Bake for 35 to 40 minutes, until the internal temperature reaches 135°F. Remove and let rest for 5 minutes.

5. Cut the salt crust away and serve tableside with the lemon wedges and olive oil for drizzling.

This cooking method will work with any whole fish. The salt seals in the moisture and aroma, so it's perfect for entertaining. Just make sure to talk with your fishmonger and ask for the freshest fish. It should have a clear eye, pink gills, and be firm to the touch. Then, for serving, the flesh should come off boneless and in chunks.

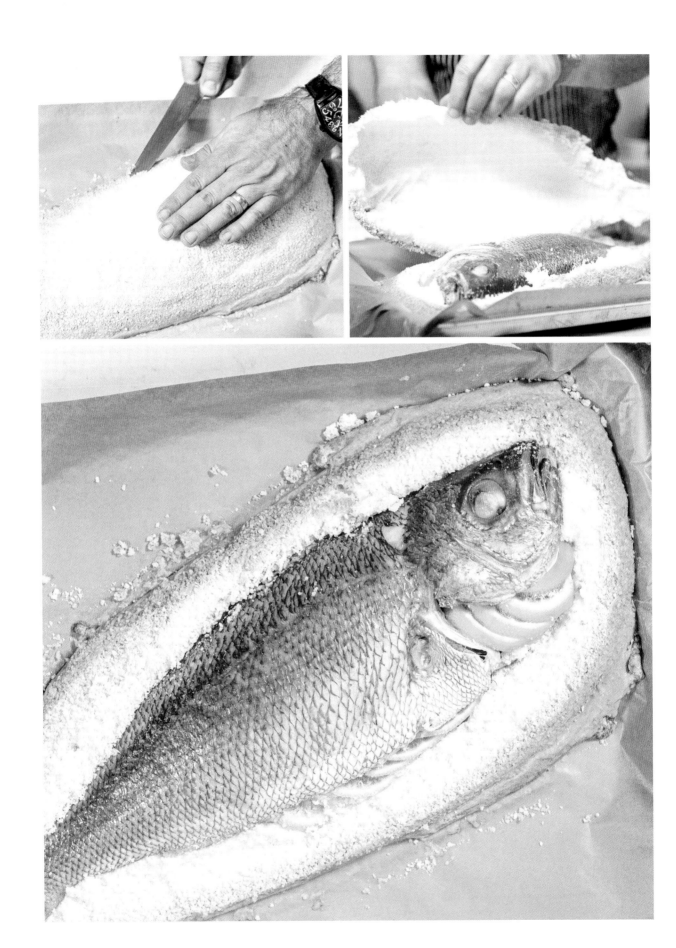

TARTIFLETTE

YIELD: 4 TO 6 SERVINGS · PREP TIME: 15 MINUTES · COOK TIME: 28 MINUTES

For Katherine, this dish checks all the boxes. The nutty fingerling potatoes are her favorite. It pairs perfectly with smoky bacon and creamy cheese and is a big pan of French goodness, which your significant other's parents will love.

½ cup bacon lardons

1 medium white onion, sliced

2 cloves garlic, sliced

1 cup dry white wine

1½ pounds fingerling potatoes, cooked and cut on the bias into ⅓-inch slices

2 cups sour cream (full fat)

1½ teaspoons kosher salt

½ teaspoon ground black pepper

1 (1-pound) wheel Reblochon or Brie, sliced into ¼-inch-wide strips

1. Preheat the oven to 425°F.

2. In a 10-inch cast-iron frying pan over medium-high heat, crisp up the bacon lardons and remove, leaving the fat in the pan.

3. Lower the heat to medium and cook the onion and garlic in the bacon fat until browned, then bring the bacon back to the party. Deglaze the pan with the wine and cook until reduced by half.

4. Toss into a mixing bowl with the sliced potatoes and sour cream. Season with the salt and pepper and stir to combine. Transfer the potato mixture to the cast-iron pan and spread into an even layer.

5. Top with the cheese strips and bake until golden and delicious, about 15 minutes. You can stick a paring knife into the potatoes to make sure they are tender.

6. Remove and let rest for 8 minutes before serving to avoid burning yourself on this gorgeous girl.

LOVE TAP   Reblochon, the traditional choice for tartiflette, is a very strong cheese, perfect for those looking for a big bang of flavor. Brie is a softer, more delicate substitute if that's your adventure.

GOING
STEADY

Delicious recipes that you'll want to make
over and over again in your relationship

OYSTERS MIGNONETTE

YIELD: 4 SERVINGS · PREP TIME: 12 MINUTES

Once you're in a steady relationship, you can start to experiment with
ingredients and recipes that are outside of your comfort zone. This is one of
them, because it might take a minute to warm up to and get comfortable with
raw oysters. Just make sure to pair your oysters with this incredibly delicious
yet simple mignonette sauce. It's the perfect wingman.

MIGNONETTE SAUCE:

1 large shallot, finely diced

½ cup ice water, or as needed

¼ cup red wine vinegar

2 tablespoons red wine

⅛ teaspoon kosher salt

12 oysters, freshly shucked

SPECIAL EQUIPMENT:

Oyster knife

1. Have on hand a small bowl into which you can fit a small
   fine-mesh strainer, using the edge of the bowl to support the
   strainer. Fill the bowl nearly to the top with ice water, then toss
   the shallots into the strainer and soak them in the ice water for
   2 to 5 minutes. Then lift the strainer out of the ice water and
   drain the shallots well.

2. In a small bowl, combine the vinegar and wine. Toss in the
   drained shallots and salt and stir until the salt is dissolved.

3. Serve the oysters on a bed of ice with the sauce alongside.

LOVE TAP Soaking the shallots in ice water removes the overpowering
smell and leaves you with a perfectly crisp texture and mild flavor.
For the red wine, you don't need to use the best bottle; just choose
something drinkable.

COCONUT POACHED COD

YIELD: 2 SERVINGS · PREP TIME: 10 MINUTES · COOK TIME: 7 MINUTES

When our relationship started getting serious, we realized how much we both love everything that comes from the sea. So any dish that includes seafood is a must for us, especially if it's cod. Here, we poach the cod in coconut milk infused with lemongrass and Thai basil to give it extra flavor and make it silky smooth, and then serve it on a bed of silky sautéed water spinach.

1 (13.5-ounce) can coconut milk

8 fresh kaffir lime leaves

6 fresh Thai basil leaves

2 chopped pencil chilies or bird's-eye chilies

2 stalks lemongrass, pounded and chopped

2 (6-ounce) cod fillets

½ teaspoon kosher salt

¼ teaspoon ground white pepper

WATER SPINACH:

1 tablespoon finely diced fresh ginger

1 teaspoon unsalted butter

1 bunch water spinach, stems removed

¼ teaspoon kosher salt

⅛ teaspoon ground black pepper

SPECIAL EQUIPMENT:

Fish spatula (optional)

1. In a saucepan wide enough to comfortably fit both cod fillets, bring the coconut milk to a soft simmer. Add the lime leaves, Thai basil, chilies, and lemongrass. Season the cod with the salt and white pepper and poach for 10 minutes per inch of thickness.

2. In a medium frying pan, toast the ginger in the butter over medium heat, then toss in the water spinach. Season with the salt and black pepper and sauté until wilted, 3 to 4 minutes.

3. Plate the spinach and top with the perfectly poached cod.

This recipe would work well with any white fish or even shellfish. Always buy based on what looks freshest, not on what the recipe calls for.

CHARRED OCTOPUS

YIELD: 2 SERVINGS · PREP TIME: 10 MINUTES, PLUS 20 MINUTES TO MARINATE · COOK TIME: 17 MINUTES

We're serious about octopus. This octopus dish even loves wine as much as we do. For your next date night, open up a bottle of white wine and sacrifice the first glass for steaming the octopus, and then enjoy the rest. (You might even like to sneak in some more of that chilled while you marinate the octopus and give it its final touch on the grill.)

LEMON AIOLI:

1 large egg

1 teaspoon Dijon mustard

½ cup extra-virgin olive oil

Grated zest and juice of ½ lemon

¼ teaspoon mild hot sauce, such as Frank's

½ teaspoon Worcestershire sauce

½ teaspoon kosher salt

MARINADE:

2 tablespoons extra-virgin olive oil

½ teaspoon paprika

½ clove garlic, minced

Juice of ½ lemon

¼ teaspoon kosher salt

⅛ teaspoon ground black pepper

CHARRED OCTOPUS:

1 cup dry white wine

Juice of ½ lemon

Juice of ½ lime

Small handful of fresh parsley, basil, or thyme sprigs

1½ pounds octopus

SPECIAL EQUIPMENT:

Steamer basket

1. Make the aioli: Blend all the ingredients in a small food processor until smooth and thick. Set aside.

2. Make the marinade: In a medium stainless-steel bowl, whisk together all the ingredients.

3. Prepare the octopus: In a medium pot, bring the wine, lemon and lime juice, and herbs to a simmer. Place the steamer basket in the pot, then add the octopus, cover the pot, and steam for 10 minutes. Remove the cooked octopus, toss it into the bowl with the marinade, and allow to cool for 20 minutes.

4. Preheat a charcoal grill to high heat.

5. Remove the octopus from the marinade; discard the marinade. Before grilling, sever the head from the body, remove the beak found in the middle of the 8 legs, and then separate the legs into individual portions.

6. Grill over the hot charcoal until crispy, 6 to 8 minutes. Serve with the aioli.

Don't make the mistake of overcooking the octopus. Just steam it for 10 minutes. No need to boil it for hours. Your date and the octopus will be much happier when you go this route. To make this meal complete, serve it with grilled potatoes. We recommend boiling whole peeled Yukon Golds until just tender, then slicing them crosswise into rounds, brushing with olive oil, and grilling them alongside the octopus.

BEEF TARTARE

YIELD: 2 SERVINGS · PREP TIME: 13 MINUTES

Since the beginning of our relationship, we've ordered tartare every time we eat out and then compare it to our own recipe, tweaking and refining it when we find a noteworthy restaurant version. There's just something about making tartare at home that makes it a date night staple. Just be sure to bring an open mind and a curious palate, as it's an acquired taste.

7 ounces beef tenderloin

4 gherkins, finely diced

2 tablespoons finely diced shallots

1 tablespoon chopped capers

¼ cup chopped fresh parsley

Juice of ½ lemon

5 splashes mild hot sauce, such as Frank's

1½ teaspoons Worcestershire sauce

1 teaspoon Dijon mustard

1 teaspoon extra-virgin olive oil

½ teaspoon kosher salt

¼ teaspoon ground black pepper

FOR GARNISH:

2 tablespoons finely sliced fresh chives

2 quail eggs

12 waffle chips (pomme gaufrette) or other sturdy potato chips

SPECIAL EQUIPMENT:

2 (3-inch) ring molds

1. Chill a medium mixing bowl and two serving plates.

2. Using a very sharp knife, dice the beef as finely as possible and toss into the chilled bowl. Add the remaining ingredients and mix to combine. Taste and adjust the seasoning if needed. It should be balanced with the acidity from the gherkins, capers, and lemon juice shining through.

3. Center the ring molds on the chilled plates and fill with the tartare. Remove the rings and cover the top half of both servings with the chives. Cut off the top of each quail eggshell, then carefully separate the yolks from the whites and return the yolks to the shells. Nestle a shell in the center of each tartare.

4. Garnish with the chips and serve.

People will try to convince you not to use tenderloin because a cheaper cut will work the same way, but we feel tenderloin works best. If your budget requires you to try a striploin or sirloin, make sure it's top quality and dice it as finely as you can. Then chop it again for the best results.

ROASTED RED PEPPER
and FETA SOUP

YIELD: 6 TO 8 SERVINGS · PREP TIME: 14 MINUTES · COOK TIME: 38 MINUTES

Every once in a while, Katherine likes to prove that she can cook. This is her go-to soup that she likes to make for Randy. Of course, it's loaded with feta, but it's legit foolproof. When she first made this dish, Randy was hooked—and still is. It goes to show you that soup can go a long way. Especially when it's this delicious.

1 cup diced carrots

1 cup diced celery

1 cup diced onions

6 cloves garlic, chopped

1 tablespoon extra-virgin olive oil

1 splash dry white wine

6 red bell peppers, roasted, peeled, and seeded

1 teaspoon kosher salt

½ teaspoon ground black pepper

2 quarts chicken or vegetable stock

2½ cups crumbled feta cheese

HERB OIL:

¼ cup chopped fresh chives

¼ cup chopped fresh dill fronds

¼ cup chopped fresh parsley

¼ cup chili-infused extra-virgin olive oil

Grated zest and juice of ½ lemon

½ teaspoon kosher salt

¼ teaspoon ground black pepper

1. In a stockpot over medium heat, sauté the carrots, celery, onions, and garlic in the olive oil until the vegetables have softened and a small amount of color has formed on the bottom of the pot.

2. Deglaze the pot with the wine, then add the roasted peppers, salt, pepper, and stock. Simmer for 30 minutes.

3. Meanwhile, make the herb oil: Combine all the ingredients in a small mixing bowl.

4. Pour the soup into a large blender, add the feta cheese, and blend until velvety smooth. If your blender isn't large enough to safely blend all of the soup, work in batches. Adjust the seasoning if needed.

5. Serve while frothy, garnished with the herb oil.

Be sure to blend the feta cheese into the soup to give it body and soul and get that perfect consistency you're after.

CHEESE FONDUE

YIELD: 2 TO 4 SERVINGS · PREP TIME: 9 MINUTES · COOK TIME: 12 MINUTES

Since we started dating, we've loved to do a weekly grazing date, and this has become one of our favorite recipes for it. It's a great way to clean out the fridge and use up all of those cheeses. Plus, it makes date night fun and interactive.

¼ cup dry white wine

½ ounce Kirsch

½ ounce brandy

1 cup shredded aged white cheddar cheese

1 cup shredded Emmental cheese

1 cup shredded Gruyère cheese

1 tablespoon cornstarch

½ teaspoon kosher salt

¼ teaspoon ground white pepper

⅛ teaspoon ground nutmeg

1 teaspoon fresh lemon juice

Crusty bread, for serving

1. In a medium heavy-bottomed pot, bring the wine, Kirsch, and brandy to a simmer.

2. In a mixing bowl, toss the cheeses with the cornstarch until evenly coated. Add to the simmering wine mixture and stir over low heat until melted. If you have a fondue pot, transfer the melted cheese mixture to the fondue pot and set to low heat to maintain the perfect consistency. If you don't have a fondue pot, you can leave the heavy-bottomed pot on the stove and hover or simply reheat the cheese mixture when it becomes too thick and cool.

3. Season the fondue with the salt, white pepper, and nutmeg. Finish with the lemon juice and serve with your favorite crusty bread.

Quality cheese is important. However, this is an adaptable fondue recipe, and the types of cheeses can be substituted to your liking. It's a great way to clean out an overflowing cheese drawer. Instead of bread, try serving the fondue with roasted vegetables. For example, you can take a whole head of cauliflower, rub it with olive oil, season it with za'atar, and then roast it. The roasted florets are made for dipping into cheese fondue.

SPICY VODKA PENNE

YIELD: 4 TO 6 SERVINGS • PREP TIME: 12 MINUTES • COOK TIME: 55 MINUTES

We don't think there's any problem that pasta can't fix. A nice comforting bowl of this spicy vodka penne will have your partner asking for this pasta week after week.

½ cup chopped onions

2 cloves garlic, minced

2 tablespoons pepperoncini chilies in oil, or to taste

3 tablespoons extra-virgin olive oil

¼ cup tomato paste

2 ounces vodka

1 (14-ounce) can whole peeled tomatoes, crushed

1 teaspoon kosher salt, divided

1 cup heavy cream

12 ounces penne pasta

1½ cups grated Parmigiano-Reggiano cheese

14 leaves fresh micro basil, or 7 fresh basil leaves, torn

1 (8-ounce) ball burrata cheese

1. In a medium saucepan over medium heat, sauté the onions, garlic, and chilies in the olive oil until translucent and soft. Add the tomato paste and pan-fry, stirring constantly, until the paste is lightly toasted. Deglaze with the vodka and cook until reduced by three-quarters.

2. Add the tomatoes with their juices and ½ teaspoon of the salt and continue cooking until reduced by half. Pour in the cream and simmer gently for 15 minutes, or until the sauce is thick.

3. Bring a large pot of water to a boil and add the remaining ½ teaspoon of salt. Boil the pasta in the salted water until it is not quite al dente. Reserve about 1 cup of the pasta cooking water, then drain the pasta.

4. Add the drained pasta to the sauce along with ½ cup of the reserved pasta water. Simmer the pasta and sauce for 4 to 5 minutes, until the pasta is cooked through. Kill the heat and add the Parmigiano-Reggiano. Adjust the seasoning and the consistency with more pasta water, if needed.

5. Plate the pasta and garnish with the basil and dollops of the burrata.

LOVE TAP Always reserve some pasta cooking water and pull the pasta early, when it's slightly underdone; it will finish cooking in the sauce. Let the sauce hold the pasta's hand; when you allow pasta to finish cooking in the sauce, you end up with the most flavorful pasta. If the sauce becomes dry before the pasta is perfectly cooked, simply wet the sauce with a bit of the reserved pasta water.

GOLDEN BEET CARPACCIO

YIELD: 2 TO 4 SERVINGS · PREP TIME: 10 MINUTES · COOK TIME: 45 MINUTES

Show your date that you don't skip a beat with this gorgeous pescatarian carpaccio. Beets are our vegetarian play on this dish that is normally reserved for beef. The acidity of the white anchovies cuts the sweetness of the beets, so this twist really shakes things up in a delicious way. Not to mention, Katherine's love language is beets, so Randy pulls out this recipe for special occasions. Every time he makes this dish, it puts a smile on her face. We hope it will do the same for your person.

BEETS:

6 to 8 medium golden beets

½ teaspoon kosher salt

DRESSING:

½ cup fresh parsley sprigs

½ cup sliced fresh chives

2 cloves garlic, peeled

1 tablespoon chopped fresh ginger

1½ teaspoons Dijon mustard

2 tablespoons dry white or rosé wine

1½ tablespoons red wine vinegar

Grated zest and juice of 1 lime

¼ cup extra-virgin olive oil

FOR GARNISH:

1 cup watercress or arugula

1 (6-ounce) ball burrata cheese, chopped

1 (1-ounce) tin white anchovies (aka boquerones)

½ teaspoon flaky sea salt

¼ teaspoon ground black pepper

1. Put the beets in a medium pot, cover with water, and season with the salt. Bring to a gentle simmer and cook for 45 minutes, or until the beets are tender. Drain and let cool. Peel and slice thinly.

2. Make the dressing: Place all the ingredients in a blender and blend until smooth.

3. Lay the beet slices on a plate as for carpaccio, overlapping them slightly and completely covering the surface of the plate. Top with the watercress and drizzle on the dressing. Garnish with the burrata, anchovies, flaky salt, and pepper.

KARTÖFFELCHEN

YIELD: 4 SERVINGS · PREP TIME: 6 MINUTES, PLUS TIME FOR POTATOES TO COOL
COOK TIME: 20 MINUTES

This is a classic German side that Katherine enjoyed growing up, so we wanted to share her roots with you. It's usually made with baby yellow-fleshed potatoes pulled from the ground just before dinner, but for us, yellow fingerling potatoes do the trick. If you're looking to step up your side game, this recipe will do just that.

1 pound yellow fingerling potatoes, scrubbed

2 cups chicken or vegetable stock

2 cloves garlic, peeled

1½ teaspoons kosher salt, divided

¼ cup (½ stick) unsalted butter

¼ cup panko breadcrumbs

¼ teaspoon ground black pepper

1 tablespoon chopped fresh parsley, for garnish

1. Put the potatoes, stock, garlic, and 1 teaspoon of the salt in a medium saucepan. Simmer gently until the potatoes are almost tender, about 15 minutes, depending on the exact size of the potatoes. Turn off the heat and let them cool in the stock before continuing to Step 2. Once cool, drain the potatoes and pat dry.

2. Melt the butter in a sauté pan, then add the breadcrumbs, remaining ½ teaspoon of salt, and pepper and toast the breadcrumbs until golden, about 4 minutes. Add the potatoes and toss to coat in the breadcrumbs.

3. Garnish with the parsley and serve.

LOVE TAP Use the freshest yellow-fleshed potatoes you can find to bring out that earthy flavor.

MARRY ME
SALADS

Tasty, fresh salads that will make you say,
"I do"

GUSTO'S KALE SALAD

If you follow us on Instagram or TikTok, you know that we love a good date night on the town. One of our favorite places to go is Gusto 101 in Toronto. If you're from Toronto, we can just about guarantee that you've ordered Gusto's famous kale salad. Then we decided, why not save some money and make this fan favorite at home? So Randy took on the challenge, and let's just say his version does not disappoint. Get ready for your new favorite kale salad that will have you thinking forever with your special someone.

1 bunch lacinato kale (aka black, Tuscan, or dinosaur kale)

Juice of 1 lemon

2 tablespoons extra-virgin olive oil

½ cup pine nuts, toasted

½ cup dried black currants (aka Zante currants or Corinth raisins)

½ cup grated pecorino cheese

¼ teaspoon ground black pepper

Shaved Parmigiano-Reggiano cheese, for garnish

1. Remove the stems from the kale and slice the kale crosswise as thinly as possible.

2. In a large bowl, combine the lemon juice and olive oil. Add the kale, massage it until the leaves are becoming soft and tender, and set aside for 5 minutes to soften further.

3. Add the pine nuts and currants to the bowl and toss to combine with the kale. Next, add the pecorino and pepper and toss again. Divide between two plates, garnish with Parmigiano-Reggiano, and serve.

LOVE TAP Lacinato kale is a very tough green, so cut it as thinly as possible. It doesn't immediately wilt once dressed, so it's great for a gathering, as it can be plated before your date arrives. It actually gets better with time, just like a good relationship.

When it comes to pine nuts, we recommend toasting them in a frying pan on the stovetop so you can keep an eye on them and make sure they don't burn.

TEN-VEGETABLE SLAW *with* PEANUT-LIME DRESSING

YIELD: 2 SERVINGS · PREP TIME: 20 MINUTES · COOK TIME: 5 MINUTES

Just like a relationship, you can get bored with salads or fall into a bit of a slump. We're here to help you keep things interesting with this Asian-inspired slaw. It's clean and refreshing, and the flavors and textures add a zing to every bite. This recipe just might light the forever flame in your relationship.

DRESSING:

1 tablespoon toasted sesame oil

1 tablespoon natural rice vinegar

Juice of 2 limes

2 teaspoons soy sauce

1 teaspoon fish sauce

1½ teaspoons smooth salted peanut butter

¼ teaspoon kosher salt

⅛ teaspoon ground black pepper

SLAW:

½ cup thinly sliced fennel

½ cup thinly sliced cabbage

½ cup thinly sliced carrots

½ cup thinly sliced cucumbers

½ cup julienned radishes

¼ cup julienned candy cane beets

¼ cup sliced green onions

¼ cup sliced snap peas (aka sugar snap peas)

2 tablespoons julienned fresh ginger

SPECIAL EQUIPMENT:

Mandoline (optional)

FOR GARNISH:

½ cup very thin strips gold potatoes, fried until crispy

½ cup very thin strips sweet potatoes, fried until crispy

¼ cup fresh cilantro leaves

¼ cup fresh mint leaves

2 tablespoons organic marigold petals or other edible flowers

1. In a medium mixing bowl, whisk together all the dressing ingredients until smooth.

2. Put all the slaw ingredients in a large bowl, then pour the dressing over them and toss to coat.

3. Mound the slaw high on two plates. Garnish with the crispy gold and sweet potatoes, cilantro, mint, and marigolds.

This is a clean-out-your-fridge kind of salad. You can add to the list of vegetables or make substitutions. The dressing brings it all together, no matter what you use. A mandoline makes quick work of thinly slicing all the vegetables for the slaw, but you can use a sharp knife instead if you want to practice your knife skills. Don't forget the garnishes. They provide texture, flavor, and color and make this slaw extra-memorable (and the marrying type).

CURLY ENDIVE
with MASHED POTATO VINAIGRETTE

YIELD: 4 TO 6 SERVINGS · PREP TIME: 12 MINUTES · COOK TIME: 15 MINUTES

Some of the best recipes to share with someone you are getting to know more closely are the ones passed down from generation to generation in your family. There's nothing more personal than that. This mashed potato vinaigrette is a beloved recipe from Katherine's family. Her Omee (grandmother) made this old-school classic; it was a staple in her household growing up, and now it's a favorite in ours. With an exceptional texture and flavor, it brings elegance to the simplest green salads. Impress your date with this salad dressing and make your own memories and traditions.

VINAIGRETTE:
(MAKES ½ CUP)

1 medium yellow-flesh potato, such as Yukon Gold, peeled and cut into 1½-inch chunks

¼ cup extra-virgin olive oil

2 tablespoons white wine vinegar

1 teaspoon granulated sugar

⅓ sweet onion, finely diced

¼ teaspoon kosher salt

⅛ teaspoon ground black pepper

1 head curly endive or chicory, washed, dried, and chopped

1. Fill a medium saucepan halfway with water and drop in the potato chunks. Set over high heat and boil the potatoes until tender, about 6 minutes, then drain, transfer to a bowl, and mash with a fork.

2. Add the rest of the vinaigrette ingredients to the mashed potato and mix with the fork until combined. The texture will be slightly chunky.

3. Toss with the salad greens and serve with a smile.

LOVE TAP — Curly endive is the superior green for this salad. If you can't find it, chicory will work. You're looking for a bitter green with some backbone that can stand up to the weighty potato vinaigrette.

PEACH *and* ENDIVE
SALAD *for* TWO

YIELD: 2 SERVINGS · PREP TIME: 8 MINUTES · COOK TIME: 4 MINUTES

The best salads are meant to be shared. The next time you're looking to impress your date, try this salad for two. Grab your forks and dive into it together.

3 heads Belgian endive, root ends trimmed and leaves separated

2 peaches or pears, sliced

½ cup crumbled extra-sharp cheddar or blue cheese

2 tablespoons very finely sliced fresh chives

½ cup raw walnut pieces

2 tablespoons extra-virgin olive oil

¼ teaspoon flaky sea salt

⅛ teaspoon ground black pepper

2 tablespoons maple syrup

Juice of ½ lemon

1. Arrange the endive leaves cup side up on a large plate and top with the peach slices, cheese, and most of the chives.

2. In a small frying pan over medium-low heat, toast the walnuts in the olive oil for 4 minutes, or until golden. Season with the salt and pepper.

3. Dress the salad with the maple syrup and lemon juice. Garnish with the remaining chives and toasted walnuts and enjoy.

Belgian endive is a great green to have around. It lasts for weeks and has an incredible flavor and crunch. It does come across as a little bitter, so don't be afraid to use the maple syrup to sweeten the deal. Look to the season when selecting your fruit: use peaches in summer, or swap them for pears in the cooler months. For the cheese, a nice three-year cheddar will lend the sharp bite you're looking for.

RANCH ICEBERG WEDGE SALAD

YIELD: 2 SERVINGS · PREP TIME: 12 MINUTES (NOT INCLUDING TIME TO COOK BACON)
COOK TIME: 9 MINUTES

Topped with a tasty homemade ranch dressing, crunchy toasted breadcrumbs, radishes, bacon, and blue cheese, this classic steakhouse salad will get your relationship moving in a more serious direction.

RANCH DRESSING:
(MAKES ABOUT 1 CUP)

½ cup plain kefir or buttermilk

¼ cup sour cream

2 tablespoons extra-virgin olive oil

1 tablespoon fresh lemon juice

2 tablespoons chopped fresh chives

2 tablespoons chopped fresh dill

2 tablespoons chopped fresh parsley

½ teaspoon kosher salt

½ teaspoon ground black pepper

WEDGE SALAD:

1 head iceberg lettuce

1 tablespoon extra-virgin olive oil

¼ cup panko breadcrumbs

¼ teaspoon kosher salt

⅛ teaspoon ground black pepper

6 radishes, thinly sliced

6 slices bacon, cooked until crispy and torn into 1-inch pieces

¼ cup crumbled blue cheese

1. Make the dressing: Put all the ingredients in a jar and shake well. Set aside.

2. Cut two 2-inch steaks from the head of iceberg. Set each one on a plate. Cover each lettuce steak with ¼ cup of the dressing, allowing it to flow into the cracks.

3. Toast the breadcrumbs: Heat the olive oil and breadcrumbs in a small saucepan over low heat. Season with the salt and pepper and toss until golden, about 5 minutes; set aside and leave in the pan to keep warm.

4. Evenly top the dressed lettuce steaks with the radishes, bacon, and blue cheese. Garnish with the toasted breadcrumbs for extra crunch.

LOVE TAP

Just because it's called a wedge salad doesn't mean the lettuce has to be cut into triangles. It's much easier to build a salad on a flat surface, so cut your iceberg accordingly. The leftover dressing will keep for up to 5 days in the refrigerator.

PANZANELLA *with* CHARRED GREEN ONIONS

YIELD: 4 SERVINGS · PREP TIME: 12 MINUTES · COOK TIME: 1 MINUTE

During tomato season, we try to eat as many tomatoes as possible, and this salad helps us do just that. Plus, this recipe is a great way to use up extra bread.

⅓ cup plus 1 tablespoon extra-virgin olive oil, divided

1 bunch green onions, root ends trimmed

¼ cup red wine vinegar

1½ teaspoons kosher salt

½ teaspoon ground black pepper

3 medium heirloom tomatoes, cut into large chunks

½ pint heirloom cherry tomatoes, cut in half

1 cucumber, cut into large chunks

½ medium red onion, sliced

1 cup fresh basil leaves

2 day-old ciabatta buns, torn into 1-inch pieces

1. In a large frying pan, heat 1 tablespoon of the olive oil over high heat until it's just beginning to smoke.

2. Pat the green onions dry and gently lay them in the hot oil away from you. Now don't touch them. Let them get good and charred on all sides. It should only take 1 minute. Remove and chop into 1-inch pieces.

3. In a large mixing bowl, combine the remaining ⅓ cup of olive oil with the vinegar, salt, and pepper. Put the tomatoes, cucumber, onion, basil, and bread in the bowl and toss to coat.

4. Adjust the seasoning if needed and serve.

This is a seasonal salad, so the tomatoes need to be at their peak to make it pop. Look for the freshest tomatoes you can find, preferably those tasty heirloom varieties. The charred green onions add some complexity to this simple beauty.

TARRAGON MUSTARD CITRUS SALAD

YIELD: 2 SERVINGS · PREP TIME: 15 MINUTES

Let's just say this salad is almost as beautiful as your partner surely is. The way the fruit is segmented makes it a real showstopper on the plate. Yes, it does take a lot of time to prepare, but it results in something so special, and pairing it with the mustard emulsion just might let your partner know your next move: popping the question! As you make this dish, they'll be waiting in anticipation.

1 navel orange

1 red grapefruit

1 pink pomelo

12 fresh tarragon leaves, torn

1 teaspoon Dijon mustard

3 tablespoons extra-virgin olive oil

½ teaspoon kosher salt

⅛ teaspoon ground black pepper

1. Chill two serving plates.

2. Cut the top and bottom off all the fruit. Then peel the citrus, making sure to cut away all the bitter white pith. Segment the fruit over a bowl to collect all the juice, trying not to get any pith or membrane, then squeeze the remaining skeleton to extract the remaining juice. Pour the juice captured in the bowl into a small food processor, holding back the segments.

3. Add the tarragon, mustard, olive oil, salt, and pepper to the food processor and blend until emulsified.

4. Pour onto the chilled plates and lay the fruit segments on top.

You can prep all the fruit in advance to save time on the evening of your date.

BIG SALAD, LITTLE STEAK

YIELD: 2 SERVINGS · PREP TIME: 10 MINUTES, PLUS 45 MINUTES TO TEMPER STEAK
COOK TIME: 12 MINUTES

This dish wins Katherine over every time Randy makes it for her. Be sure to go with a quality steak and a vibrant, crunchy salad green to show your partner just how special to you they are.

LITTLE STEAK:

1 (12-ounce) boneless striploin (aka New York strip steak), about 1½ inches thick

1 teaspoon kosher salt

¼ teaspoon ground black pepper

1 tablespoon extra-virgin olive oil

DRESSING:

1½ teaspoons Dijon mustard

1½ teaspoons honey

2 tablespoons red wine vinegar

6 tablespoons extra-virgin olive oil

1 teaspoon kosher salt

1 teaspoon ground black pepper

3 tablespoons grated Parmigiano-Reggiano cheese

BIG SALAD:

1 big bowl of mixed greens (see Love Tap)

¼ cup torn fresh dill fronds

1. Set the steak on the counter to temper for 45 minutes.

2. Preheat a large cast-iron frying pan over medium-high heat. Season the steak with the salt and pepper.

3. When the pan is piping hot, pour in the olive oil, jack up the heat to high, and set the steak in the pan. Sear the steak without moving for 3 to 4 minutes to create a crust, then flip and sear for another 3 to 4 minutes. Kill the heat and let rest in the pan until the internal temperature hits 125°F. Remove from the pan and rest for another 6 to 8 minutes. After the final resting, the steak will be medium-rare.

4. While the steak is resting, make the dressing: Put all the ingredients in a small bowl and lightly whisk to combine; set aside.

5. Stack the salad greens and dill high on two plates and dress with as much of the dressing as you like.

6. Slice the steak and tuck it in beside the salad.

A good rule of thumb is to rest steak for as long as it takes to cook. For the mixed greens, butterhead, endive, radicchio, romaine, and watercress all work well.

LENTIL, FETA, *and* PARSLEY SALAD

YIELD: 2 SERVINGS · PREP TIME: 10 MINUTES, PLUS 15 MINUTES FOR LENTILS TO COOL
COOK TIME: 14 MINUTES

Katherine believes parsley makes an excellent salad, especially when she marries it with hearty lentils and tangy feta cheese. So this salad has become her masterpiece, and it has Randy saying, "Let's enjoy this together forever." It's similar to tabbouleh, but Katherine replaces the traditional bulgur with lentils for sustenance.

1½ cups brown lentils

2 cups vegetable stock

Grated zest and juice of 1 lemon

3 tablespoons extra-virgin olive oil

1 teaspoon kosher salt

½ teaspoon ground black pepper

2 cups roughly chopped fresh curly parsley

1 cup crumbled feta cheese

1. Put the lentils in a medium saucepan and top with the vegetable stock. Simmer gently over medium heat until just tender, 12 to 14 minutes.

2. While the lentils are simmering, make the dressing: In a medium serving bowl, mix the lemon zest and juice with the olive oil, salt, and pepper.

3. Drain the lentils and immediately add to the bowl with the dressing.

4. Toss to coat and set aside for 15 minutes, stirring occasionally, or until cool.

5. Add the parsley and feta to the lentils and toss. Adjust the seasoning if needed and plate.

GROWING OLD
TOGETHER

Classic dishes that will stay in your family
for generations

BOEUF BOURGUIGNON

YIELD: 6 TO 8 SERVINGS · PREP TIME: 20 MINUTES · COOK TIME: 2 HOURS

It's no secret that marriage is hard work, but there's not much that can't be solved over a comforting bowl of beef stew. This particularly delicious version is layered with flavor, using smoked lardons, carrots, mushrooms, pearl onions, and French Burgundy wine, which gives the stew its name. Think of this classic dish as a therapist, because it'll help you and your partner fall in love all over again.

2 cups bacon lardons, preferably double smoked

1 (4-pound) boneless picanha steak (aka sirloin or rump cap or coulotte), cut into 2-inch pieces

1 teaspoon kosher salt

1 teaspoon ground black pepper

2 tablespoons unsalted butter

1 carrot, finely diced

4 shallots, finely diced

12 cloves garlic, peeled

4 sprigs fresh thyme

2 bay leaves, dried or fresh

2 tablespoons tomato paste

3 tablespoons all-purpose flour

1 (750-ml) bottle red Burgundy wine or other dry red wine of choice, preferably pinot noir

4 cups beef stock

2 cups pearl onions, peeled

2 cups small cremini mushrooms, cleaned

12 baby carrots

Mashed potatoes, for serving

Chopped fresh parsley, for garnish

1. In a large Dutch oven over medium heat, cook the bacon lardons until the fat is rendered and the lardons are crispy, 4 to 5 minutes. Remove from the pot with a slotted spoon, leaving the fat in the pot.

2. Season the steak with the salt and pepper and sear in the bacon fat, still over medium heat, until it has a nice crust and a golden brown color, 3 to 4 minutes per side. Remove from the pot and set aside.

3. Reduce the heat to medium-low and drop in the butter, carrot, shallots, and garlic cloves; cook until they start to color, about 5 minutes. Add the herbs, tomato paste, and flour and gently toast over low heat for 5 minutes, stirring often. Next, deglaze the pot with the entire bottle of wine.

4. Return the picanha and bacon to the pot, increase the heat to medium-high, and simmer vigorously until the wine is reduced by half. Pour in the stock and cover the pot. Lower the heat and gently simmer for 1 hour 20 minutes, or until the beef is fork-tender.

5. About 10 minutes before the meat is done, add the onions, mushrooms, and carrots and simmer for another 10 minutes, or until the carrots are tender but still firm. Taste and adjust the seasoning if needed.

6. Plate with mashed potatoes, top with chopped parsley, and serve.

Use a nice bottle of red wine for this recipe to maximize the flavor. Plus, if you buy an extra bottle, it pairs perfectly with the dish once it's ready to enjoy. To make it easier to peel the pearl onions, blanch them in water for 10 seconds and then shock them in ice water for 1 minute.

CHICKEN PERNOD

YIELD: 4 SERVINGS · PREP TIME: 10 MINUTES · COOK TIME: 40 MINUTES

This recipe was passed down to Katherine by her Omee (grandmother). Katherine grew up enjoying this dish on a weekly basis. Thankfully, she was happy to share it with Randy to keep the tradition alive. It's one of our favorite chicken dishes due in large part to the Pernod, a French anise-flavored liqueur that gives it a magical flavor (so magical that Katherine laps up the sauce with a spoon). We love walking down memory lane whenever we whip this up for dinner.

4 to 6 bone-in, skin-on chicken thighs

1 teaspoon kosher salt, divided

1 teaspoon ground black pepper, divided

2 tablespoons extra-virgin olive oil, divided

12 cloves garlic, sliced

12 cipollini onions, halved horizontally and peeled

½ cup dry white wine

¾ cup Pernod

¾ cup chicken stock

1 medium head fennel, cut from top to bottom into ½-inch-thick pieces

Cooked rice or potatoes, for serving

1. Season the chicken thighs with ¾ teaspoon each of the salt and pepper.

2. Preheat a large braiser or deep-sided cast-iron frying pan over medium-high heat, then pour in 1 tablespoon of the olive oil. Sear the seasoned chicken thighs skin side down until shattering crisp, about 4 minutes. Turn the chicken over and add the garlic and onions. When the aromatics begin to brown, deglaze the pan with the white wine and cook until the liquid is reduced by half, about 2 minutes.

3. Add the Pernod and reduce by half, then pour in the chicken stock. Simmer gently for 18 to 20 minutes, until the chicken reaches an internal temperature of 160°F.

4. Drizzle the fennel with the remaining tablespoon of olive oil and season with the remaining ¼ teaspoon each of salt and pepper. Then, in a separate large frying pan over medium heat, gently sear the seasoned fennel. When it has a nice crust on one side, turn it and sear the other side, about 4 minutes per side.

5. Serve the chicken and fennel with rice or potatoes and top with the pan sauce.

Be sure to use chicken thighs for the win! They are a better option than breasts not only financially but flavorwise as well.

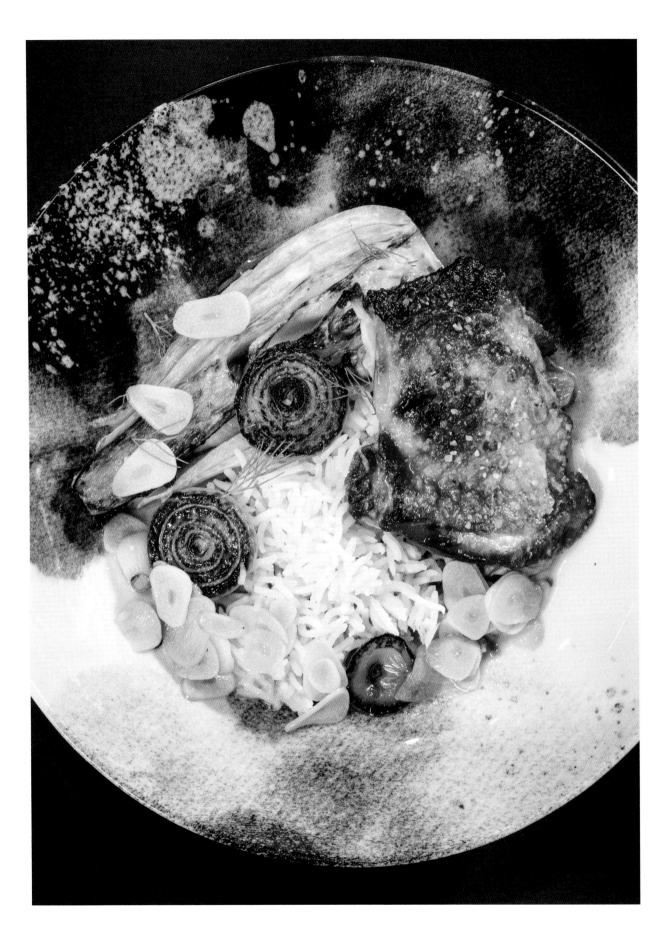

CHEESE DRAWER RISOTTO *with* SUN-DRIED TOMATO PESTO

YIELD: 2 SERVINGS · PREP TIME: 10 MINUTES (NOT INCLUDING TIME TO PREPARE GARNISHES)
COOK TIME: 22 MINUTES

Since the beginning of our relationship, our cheese drawer has been constantly overflowing. Katherine loves cheese and can't resist trying a new type or getting more of her favorites (the list is at twenty cheeses and growing). So for us, this risotto is a clean-out-your-fridge kind of meal. It lets us make the most of the bits and pieces of cheese that have been left behind, giving these little gems the perfect final resting place.

RISOTTO:

3 cups chicken or vegetable stock

3 tablespoons unsalted butter

½ cup diced shallots

1 clove garlic, chopped

1 cup Arborio rice

½ cup dry white wine

1 cup shredded or grated cheese(s) of choice (such as mozzarella, Gruyère, cheddar, Parmesan, and/or pecorino)

Juice of ½ lemon

SUN-DRIED TOMATO PESTO:

8 sun-dried tomatoes, packed in oil (reserve oil)

1 clove garlic, peeled

2 fresh basil leaves

1 tablespoon grated Parmigiano-Reggiano cheese

3 tablespoons oil from the sun-dried tomatoes

FOR GARNISH:

2 tablespoons Sun-Dried Tomato Pesto (from above)

8 slices pancetta, baked until crispy

8 fresh sage leaves, fried in olive oil until crispy

1. Make the risotto: Heat the stock in a medium saucepan over medium heat. Once at a bare simmer, keep over low heat at the back of the stove.

2. In a separate medium saucepan, melt the butter over medium heat. Add the shallots and garlic and cook until the shallots are translucent, about 4 minutes. Add the rice and toast slightly, 1 to 2 minutes, then deglaze the pan with the wine and cook until it is reduced by half.

3. Add the hot stock one ladle at a time and stir until the rice has absorbed the liquid. Repeat this process over and over again for 14 minutes. This will keep the rice light and creamy.

4. While stirring, add the cheese little by little until fully melted. Finish with the lemon juice and adjust the seasoning if needed, keeping in mind that the pancetta will add a salty element.

5. Make the sun-dried tomato pesto: Blend all the ingredients in a mini food processor until you have a smooth paste.

6. Transfer the risotto to two large pasta bowls. Garnish with the pesto, crispy pancetta, and fried sage leaves.

LOVE TAP If you are serving multiple courses, make the risotto in advance, cooking it about 70 percent of the way through. The rice should still be a little raw and crunchy on the inside. Let cool on a sheet pan and then finish cooking it just before serving. For the crispy pancetta, we recommend baking it on a nonstick sheet pan in a preheated 375°F oven using the convection setting for about 8 minutes. For the fried sage leaves, heat up 1 tablespoon of olive oil in a small frying pan over medium heat and fry for 4 to 6 minutes.

CAULIFLOWER CHICKEN POT PIE

YIELD: 6 TO 8 SERVINGS · PREP TIME: 25 MINUTES, PLUS 30 MINUTES TO REST DOUGH
AND 30 MINUTES TO COOL · COOK TIME: 1 HOUR 15 MINUTES

If you ask us, chicken pot pie should be a staple in any kitchen. It is in ours, and we like to put our own little spins on it. First, we add pureed cauliflower to the filling to make it extra-creamy and delicious (which is also a great way to sneak more veggies into your meal). Second, we bake the pie in a springform pan, which has much taller sides than the more typical choice of a pie plate. The result is a stunning presentation.

CRUST:

2¼ cups all-purpose flour

½ teaspoon kosher salt

¾ cup (1½ sticks) ice-cold unsalted butter, diced small

6 tablespoons ice water

FILLING:

Florets from ½ head cauliflower, cut into ½-inch pieces

1¼ cups milk, divided

2 cloves garlic, sliced

1 cup sliced carrots

½ cup sliced celery

⅓ cup chopped white onions

⅓ cup unsalted butter, plus extra for the springform pan

⅓ cup all-purpose flour

½ cup dry white wine

1 tablespoon Dijon mustard

1¾ cups chicken broth

1 pound cooked chicken breast, cubed

1 cup frozen green peas

1 teaspoon fresh thyme leaves

½ teaspoon kosher salt

¼ teaspoon ground black pepper

EGG WASH:

1 large egg

1 teaspoon milk

SPECIAL EQUIPMENT:

9-inch springform pan

1. Make the crust: In a food processor, pulse all the ingredients until pebbles form. Place the shaggy dough on the counter and knead into a smooth dough. Take about two-thirds of the dough and form it into a disk, then form the remaining one-third into a disk. Wrap both disks in plastic wrap and refrigerate for 30 minutes.

2. While the dough is resting, make the filling: In a medium saucepan over medium heat, steam the cauliflower in ¼ cup of the milk until tender, about 8 minutes. Using an immersion blender, blend until smooth, or carefully transfer the cauliflower and milk to a regular blender and puree.

3. In a large saucepan over medium heat, sauté the garlic, carrots, celery, and onions in the butter until softened, about 6 minutes. Add the flour and stir until toasted, another 3 minutes or so. Deglaze the pan with the wine, then add the cauliflower puree, remaining cup of milk, mustard, and chicken stock and stir to combine. Stir in the chicken, peas, and thyme. Season with the salt and pepper and simmer until the filling mixture has thickened, about 8 minutes.

4. Preheat the oven to 400°F. Grease the springform pan with butter.

5. Remove the dough from the refrigerator. Roll out the larger disk into a 16-inch circle and the smaller one into a 10-inch circle, each about ¼ inch thick.

6. Place the 16-inch dough round in the prepared pan; press it into the corners and make sure it goes all the way up the sides. Trim off any overhanging dough. Fill with the chicken mixture and top with the smaller dough round. Seal together with a soft pinch.

7. Aggressively beat the egg with the teaspoon of milk to make an egg wash. Brush the top crust with the egg wash and make 4 slits in the crust for the pie to breathe.

8. Bake for 40 to 50 minutes, until the crust is golden brown. The filling should begin to bubble and seep through the slits in the crust. Let cool for about 30 minutes before serving.

LOVE TAD We're serious about letting this pie cool before serving; scorching the roof of your mouth does not exactly set the stage for after-dinner romance. The pie can be assembled a day in advance and baked the day of for the perfect crust (because reheated crust is just never as good...).

RED WINE–BRAISED SHORT RIBS

YIELD: 4 SERVINGS · PREP TIME: 12 MINUTES · COOK TIME: 2 HOURS

Like a marriage, these braised short ribs take a long time to come together. You need to take it slow and let those flavors marry. But when they do, oh my stars, there is nothing better in this world.

4 (3-inch) short ribs

1 teaspoon kosher salt

1 teaspoon ground black pepper

1 tablespoon extra-virgin olive oil

4 cloves garlic, sliced

1 white onion, diced

1 celery stalk, finely diced

½ carrot, finely diced

1 tablespoon tomato paste

2 cups Cabernet Sauvignon wine

1 quart beef stock

6 sprigs fresh thyme

2 bay leaves, dried or fresh

FOR SERVING/GARNISH:

2 servings starchy side of choice, such as buttery noodles, mashed potatoes, polenta, or risotto

2 servings sautéed mushrooms of choice

2 crunchy dill pickles, chopped

1 handful fresh parsley, chopped

¼ cup crème fraîche or sour cream

Ground black pepper

1. Season the short ribs with the salt and pepper.

2. Place a large Dutch oven over medium-high heat and pour in the olive oil. Then add the short ribs and sear until golden. Remove the ribs from the pot and set aside, leaving the rendered fat behind.

3. Turn the heat down to medium and add the garlic, onion, celery, carrot, and tomato paste. Cook, stirring occasionally, until soft, 5 to 6 minutes. Deglaze the pot with the wine and cook until the liquid is reduced by half, about 12 minutes. Pour in the stock and add the thyme and bay leaves.

4. Return the short ribs to the pot, cover, and simmer gently for 1 hour 45 minutes, or until the meat is fork-tender.

5. Plate with your favorite starchy side and sautéed mushrooms, then top the short ribs with the pickles, parsley, and crème fraîche. Garnish with some black pepper and serve.

LOVE TAP

Everything tastes better with a bone in. So talk to your butcher and get a center-cut, 3-inch short rib. It looks amazing on the plate and is a perfect portion size for you and your beloved.

MEATBALLS
with POLENTA

YIELD: 6 TO 8 SERVINGS · PREP TIME: 15 MINUTES · COOK TIME: 40 MINUTES

After a long, busy week, there is nothing more comforting than spending a Sunday night at the table with your favorite person, enjoying tender meatballs with creamy polenta. Polenta is so underrated; all it really needs is a lot of cheese and some accompanying meatballs to hug your soul and reconnect you with your partner.

MEATBALLS:

6 cups tomato sauce, for poaching and serving

4 slices white bread (stale is best), crusts removed

¾ cup milk

¼ cup dry white wine

2 tablespoons extra-virgin olive oil

1 cup grated Parmigiano-Reggiano cheese

1 pound ground beef

1 pound ground pork

1 shallot, grated

3 cloves garlic, chopped

3 tablespoons chopped fresh parsley

2 teaspoons kosher salt

¾ teaspoon ground black pepper

POLENTA:

4½ cups chicken stock

1 cup milk

2 tablespoons unsalted butter

¾ cup fine cornmeal

1 cup shredded white cheddar cheese

½ cup grated Parmigiano-Reggiano cheese

Splash of extra-virgin olive oil

1 teaspoon kosher salt

½ teaspoon ground black pepper

1. Bring the tomato sauce to a gentle simmer in a stockpot over medium heat.

2. While the tomato sauce is heating up, make the meatball mixture: Put the bread and milk in a large mixing bowl. Tear apart and squish the bread with your hands to make a paste. Add the remaining ingredients for the meatballs. Using your hands, mix with authority until combined. Now do it again. Don't worry; this vigorous mixing will make the meatballs light and fluffy.

3. Cook a small test sample of the meat mixture and taste for seasoning, then adjust the seasoning of the rest of the meat mixture if needed.

4. Form into 1½-ounce balls and poach in the gently simmering tomato sauce until cooked through, about 35 minutes. Once the meatballs are done, remove them from the pot, reserving the sauce for plating. About 15 minutes before the meatballs are done, begin making the polenta.

5. Bring the chicken stock, milk, and butter to a gentle simmer in a large saucepan over medium heat. Whisk in the cornmeal and simmer until creamy and tender, about 12 minutes. It will be really loose at first, and that's okay; it will slowly thicken. Once it is cooked and hugs the back of a spoon, stir in the cheddar, Parmigiano-Reggiano, and olive oil. Season with the salt and pepper.

6. Plate the polenta and top with the meatballs and sauce.

Some people like to sear and then roast meatballs, but we prefer them poached. Why would you cook your balls in a dry environment when poaching makes them so much more moist and tender?

SQUID PUTTANESCA

YIELD: 2 TO 4 SERVINGS · PREP TIME: 12 MINUTES · COOK TIME: 12 MINUTES

Who wouldn't want to grow old over bowls of squid puttanesca? Puttanesca is a staple sauce in our household. The sweet tomatoes and anchovy create a heavenly flavor combination that perfectly balances the acidity of the capers and olives, which is why it pairs perfectly with squid.

5 whole U10 squids, cleaned and separated into bodies and tentacles

½ (28-ounce) can whole peeled tomatoes, smashed

1½ teaspoons sliced fresh pencil chilies or bird's-eye chilies

5 cloves garlic, smashed and sliced

½ anchovy, sliced

2 tablespoons extra-virgin olive oil

2 tablespoons capers

1 cup mixed green and black olives, pitted and halved

¼ cup dry white wine

½ teaspoon kosher salt

½ teaspoon ground black pepper

8 fresh basil leaves

Crostini or fresh bread, for serving

1. Cut each squid body down on one side and score from the inside every ⅛ inch, being careful not to cut through the entire body. Cutting about 80 percent of the way through allows for more flavor penetration and allows the squids to cook evenly.

2. Place the squid bodies and tentacles along with the tomatoes and chilies in a bowl and massage. Set aside to marinate for 10 minutes.

3. In a large braiser or deep-sided cast-iron frying pan over medium heat, toast the garlic and anchovy in the olive oil. Add the capers and olives and sauté until the garlic begins to color, about 3 minutes, then deglaze the pan with the wine. Cook until the wine has evaporated, then add the squid mixture.

4. Toss and cook gently until the squids turn white and firm up, about 4 minutes.

5. Season with the salt and pepper, top with the basil, and serve with crostini or fresh bread.

LOVE TAP When you're buying the squids, ask for the bodies (aka tubes) and tentacles. U10 means there are 10 squid bodies in a pound. We prefer this larger size because it makes for a better bite.

Scoring the squids allows them to suck up as much flavor as possible, so don't skip that step. Please do not overcook them, and use a delicate touch when turning them in the pan.

Try making your own crostini to garnish this dish. All you have to do is slice and toast a baguette with olive oil and chopped fresh parsley.

SPATCHCOCKED ROAST CHICKEN
with SALSA VERDE

YIELD: 2 TO 4 SERVINGS · PREP TIME: 10 MINUTES · COOK TIME: 45 MINUTES

This roast chicken recipe is one that will stand the test of time. It's so versatile, and every bit of the bird can be used in so many other dishes. This is one of our favorite ways to enjoy chicken because the spatchcock technique allows the chicken to cook evenly and gives it more surface to render the fat, get nice and crispy, and lock in all the flavor. Let's just say it'll definitely put a smile on your partner's face whenever you make it.

1 (3- to 4-pound) whole chicken

1 tablespoon extra-virgin olive oil

2 teaspoons kosher salt

1 teaspoon ground black pepper

SALSA VERDE:
(MAKES 2 CUPS)

4 handfuls fresh curly parsley, washed well

1 bunch green onions, green parts only

2 cloves garlic, peeled

2 tablespoons capers

¼ cup gherkins

¼ red chili pepper

½ cup extra-virgin olive oil

3 tablespoons red wine vinegar

1 tablespoon kosher salt

1 tablespoon ground black pepper

1. Preheat the oven to 375°F.

2. Spatchcock the chicken: Place the chicken breast side down on a work surface. Cutting first on one side, then the other, remove the spine of the bird with kitchen scissors. (Once you're more adept and understand chicken anatomy, you can use a large knife for this task.) Turn the chicken over and press down on the breastbone to flatten the chicken.

3. Give the bird an olive oil rubdown and season every inch with the salt and pepper.

4. Place the chicken skin side up in a large cast-iron frying pan and slide the pan into the oven. Roast for 45 minutes, or until the internal temperature in the breast reaches 155°F. Remove and let rest for 10 minutes.

5. Meanwhile, make the salsa verde: Put all the ingredients in a blender and blend until smooth.

6. Plate the chicken and serve with the salsa.

Make sure to double-wash your parsley. This salsa is full of flavor, so don't ruin it with a few specks of dirt. You might eat the entire quantity of salsa with bread before the chicken is done (but try not to) or all of it with the chicken. But if you don't and have some left over, cover it and store it in the fridge for up to 2 weeks.

GET OUT OF JAIL
FREE CARD

Dishes that will get you back on
your partner's good side in no time

WINE *and* CHEESE

YIELD: 2 TO 4 SERVINGS • PREP TIME: 5 MINUTES, PLUS 30 MINUTES TO TEMPER CHEESES

Is wine and cheese always a good idea? Yes. A beautiful charcuterie board with a nice bottle of wine is a simple meal—any day, any time. Pop into your local cheesemonger and see what they recommend. Then pop into your local wine shop and do the same. To get you started, we're sharing our favorites in the Love Tap. But know this: you can't go wrong. You can be as adventurous and elaborate as you like or as simple as you like. It all depends on what you and your partner prefer at the end of the day (or the middle of the day...).

CHEESE:

3 to 4 ounces hard cheese

3 to 4 ounces semi-hard cheese

3 to 4 ounces soft cheese

2 ounces blue cheese (optional)

A selection of accoutrements of choice

WINE:

A bottle of your favorite red, white, or sparkling

SPECIAL EQUIPMENT:

Charcuterie board

Cheese knives

Demitasse spoons

Mini bowls

1. Remove the cheeses from the refrigerator at least 30 minutes ahead of time to allow them to come to room temperature.

2. Arrange the cheeses and accoutrements in a decorative manner on your favorite board.

3. Serve with your favorite wine or bubbles.

We love a variety of cheeses, such as a firm aged Parmigiano-Reggiano, Comté, or Manchego, semi-firm cheddar or Gouda, and a soft unpasteurized cow's milk like Brie de Meaux or a Camembert. Blue cheeses, always distinctive, deserve their own category: for a more adventurous option, try Saint Agur or Roquefort; for beginners, the creamy Cambozola (or a "blue brie") is a good choice.

Also important are the "accoutrements" (accompaniments). Options include dried fruit (apricots, figs, cherries), fresh fruit (sliced apple and/or pear, figs, grapes), cured meats (fuet or Spanish jamon), nuts, honey, preserves, and fresh bread, breadsticks, or crostini.

When it comes to the wine, generally the more expensive you go, the better it tastes. But we want to leave that up to you, as everyone has their own preferences and budget. For example, Randy loves a good French pinot noir or a dry white wine, whereas Katherine is a bubbles girl. If it's a random Tuesday, she wants prosecco. If it's a weekend, she wants cava. And for a special occasion or cause for celebration, she wants to pop open the Champagne (her favorite is Laurent Perrier Rosé Champagne).

SQUID SANDWICH

YIELD: 2 SANDWICHES · PREP TIME: 5 MINUTES · COOK TIME: 3 MINUTES

We first discovered our love for squid sandwiches at our favorite restaurant in Barcelona. We adore Spain and took a trip to Barcelona very early in our relationship and then again for our honeymoon, when we fit in a visit to San Sebastián as well. During our first trip there, we visited Bar Cañete on the advice of our friend Rob Rossi, whose restaurants include Giulietta and Osteria Giulia. We returned several times during that short five-day trip and again on our honeymoon four years or so later.

2 cups extra-virgin olive oil, for frying

1½ teaspoons unsalted butter, softened

2 semolina kaiser rolls, split

2 tablespoons mayonnaise

1 whole U10 squid, cleaned and separated into bodies and tentacles

½ teaspoon paprika

¼ teaspoon ground black pepper

3 tablespoons cornstarch

½ teaspoon kosher salt

2 small handfuls watercress

1 tablespoon extra-virgin olive oil

Juice of ¼ lemon

1. In a stockpot over medium heat, heat up the olive oil to 350°F.

2. Butter the rolls and toast buttered side down in a hot cast-iron frying pan over medium heat until golden. Dress with the mayonnaise.

3. Tear up the squid tentacles into 2-inch pieces. Cut the squid body down one side to open it up. Score the underside in a crisscross pattern. Then cut into 1-inch-wide ribbons and pat dry.

4. In a mixing bowl, combine the paprika, pepper, and cornstarch. Toss the squid in the mixture until it's well coated.

5. Fry the squid until golden, about 3 minutes, then season with the salt. Stack the squid on the bottom rolls.

6. Dress the watercress with the olive oil and lemon juice, place on top of the squid, and crown the sandwiches with the top rolls.

We swapped out the sugar in this recipe for maple syrup because Randy's dad owns a sugar shack, and we love to incorporate it into our recipes whenever a little sweetness is needed.

Tête de Moine is a semi-hard cheese from Switzerland made with raw cow's milk. It comes in a cylindrical form and is cut with a special device called a cheese curler or cheese shaver into rosettes, or flowers. It's a specialty cheese, but if you can get your hands on some, you won't be disappointed. We enjoy it so much that we invested in the device used to cut it. We're serious about Tête de Moine.

FRENCH ONION SOUP-SANDWICH

YIELD: 2 SERVINGS · PREP TIME: 12 MINUTES · COOK TIME: 45 MINUTES

Who can stay mad with a bowl of French onion soup in front of them? Especially when you deconstruct it a bit and make it something new? Here, instead of getting a bowl of soup that you eat with a spoon, you get a rimmed plate covered with enough soup to soak into every single bite of the crusty, cheesy crouton. We got this idea from a *Bon Appétit* article and put our own spin on it. The next time you find yourself in hot water, whip up Randy's take on French onion soup.

2 teaspoons unsalted butter

Splash of extra-virgin olive oil

2 large sweet onions, such as Vidalia, diced

1 tablespoon maple syrup

2 tablespoons red wine vinegar

2 ounces cognac

3 cups beef stock

1 teaspoon kosher salt

½ teaspoon ground black pepper

3 sprigs fresh thyme

2 bay leaves, dried or fresh

CHEESY CROUTONS:

2 slices sourdough bread, grilled

1 clove garlic, cut in half

1 tablespoon unsalted butter, softened

6 slices provolone cheese

6 slices Gruyère cheese

12 flowers of Tête de Moine cheese (optional)

1. Heat the butter and olive oil in a medium saucepan over medium-low heat. Add the onions and sauté until translucent, then add the maple syrup and cook until deeply caramelized, about 30 minutes.

2. Deglaze with the vinegar and reduce by half.

3. Deglaze with the cognac and again reduce by half. Add the stock, salt, pepper, thyme, and bay leaves and simmer for 10 minutes. When done, taste and adjust the seasoning to your liking.

4. Meanwhile, make the cheesy croutons: Preheat the oven broiler to high. Rub the grilled bread slices with the garlic, then spread with the butter. Top with the cheese slices and flowers of Tête de Moine cheese, if using. Then broil on a sheet pan on the middle rack of the oven until the cheese is melted and golden; watch carefully to avoid burning it.

5. Divide the soup between two rimmed dinner plates (see Love Tap). Garnish with the melted cheese croutons and serve with a knife and fork.

LOVE TAP
Be sure to serve the soup on a rimmed plate to contain the soup. A plate that's about 10 inches in diameter with a 1-inch rim is ideal. The plate should be wide enough for the crouton to sit flat so that it can be cut with a knife and fork. (A soup plate or shallow bowl may also work.) This will let you get the perfect soup-to-crouton ratio in every bite.

SEARED FOIE GRAS
and VANILLA
POACHED PEAR

YIELD: 2 SERVINGS · PREP TIME: 10 MINUTES · COOK TIME: 25 MINUTES

There is no problem a high-quality foie gras can't fix—especially when it's paired with vanilla poached pear. Sear it over high heat in a dry pan until golden on both sides and let it rest. With the first bite, your significant other will forget why they were even upset in the first place.

POACHED PEAR:

1 Bosc pear, not quite fully ripe

2 tablespoons honey

1 cup Riesling wine

1 teaspoon minced fresh ginger

1 vanilla bean (about 6 inches long), split and seeds scraped

3 cardamom pods

1 tablespoon unsalted butter, softened

2 slices soft sourdough bread

2 (3-ounce) slabs foie gras

1 teaspoon kosher salt

1. Peel, halve, and core the pear. Place the pear halves in a small saucepan and add the honey, Riesling, ginger, vanilla pod and seeds, and cardamom pods. Simmer over medium heat until the pear is soft, about 15 minutes. Slide the pan off the heat and let the pear rest in the poaching liquid; you want it to be warm but not hot when ready to serve.

2. Butter the bread slices and toast buttered side down in a hot cast-iron frying pan. Remove and trim down to the size of the foie gras slabs.

3. Preheat a dry medium cast-iron frying pan over high heat. Meanwhile, score the foie gras and season with the salt.

4. When the pan is hot, place the foie gras slabs in the pan and sear until the fat starts to darken, about 2 minutes, then flip and sear the other side for an additional 2 minutes. Remove from the pan and let rest for 2 minutes.

5. Slice the pear and lay it on the toasted sourdough. Top with the foie gras and serve.

CAVIAR PIZZA FRITTA

YIELD: ONE 4-INCH PIZZA · PREP TIME: 15 MINUTES, PLUS 24 HOURS TO REST AND TEMPER DOUGH
COOK TIME: 6 MINUTES

This pizza is a Randy favorite. He is obsessed with caviar. The combination of caviar, crème fraîche, and warm pan-fried dough will have you remembering that first bite for years to come.

DOUGH:
(MAKES FOUR 6-OUNCE BALLS)

1.1 pounds pizza flour (type 00)

3 tablespoons warm water

1 (¼-ounce) package active dry yeast

1½ teaspoons maple syrup, or 1 teaspoon granulated sugar

1 cup plus 1 tablespoon cold water

1 tablespoon extra-virgin olive oil

½ teaspoon kosher salt

PIZZA:

1 (6-ounce) ball pizza dough

¼ cup extra-virgin olive oil

1 ounce sturgeon caviar

2 tablespoons crème fraîche or sour cream

SPECIAL EQUIPMENT:

Bench knife

Leave the dough out at room temperature for a minimum of 1 hour before you work it. This will make it stretch much more easily.

1. Make the dough: Dump the flour onto a clean work surface. Create a thick mound of flour, then make a well in the center. (The ring of flour around the well will serve as a wall once the wet ingredients are added.) Pour the warm water into the well, then add the yeast and maple syrup and give it a stir with your finger. Once frothy, add the cold water, olive oil, and salt and give the liquid mixture another stir with your finger. Little by little, carefully begin bringing the flour from the walls into the wet mixture, mixing with a fork. Once the mixture in the center is no longer runny, use a bench knife to work in the rest of the flour until you have a shaggy dough. Now use your hands to knead it into a smooth dough ball; you will need to work it for about 20 minutes.

2. Portion the dough into four 6-ounce pieces. Form each piece into a ball, then wrap each ball in plastic wrap. Refrigerate in an airtight container overnight or for up to 24 hours.

3. Remove one or more dough balls from the fridge (depending on how many pizzas you want to make) and set on the counter for 1 hour, or until the dough has come to room temperature.

4. Place a dough ball on a floured work surface and, using your fingers, very gently stretch out the dough until it is 4 inches in diameter, creating an edge all the way around.

5. Pour the olive oil into a medium frying pan over medium-low heat. Place the dough in the pan and fry until golden, 2 to 3 minutes, then flip and fry for another 2 to 3 minutes, until golden on both sides. Remove from the pan and let cool for a couple minutes, until no longer piping hot but still warm.

6. Spread the caviar evenly on the crust and top with small dollops of the crème fraîche.

BLOOD ORANGE SCALLOP CRUDO

YIELD: 2 SERVINGS · PREP TIME: 12 MINUTES

If your partner in crime is a seafood lover, this simple, clean dish will
get you back in their good graces in no time. Its beautiful colors—that
are almost as seductive as its delicious flavor—will definitely knock
their socks off when you set this dish in front of them.

CHIVE OIL:
(MAKES ½ CUP)

¼ cup extra-virgin olive oil

½ cup chopped fresh chives

SCALLOP CRUDO:

1 blood orange

8 ounces Hokkaido sea scallops or dry diver scallops

3 tablespoons chive oil (from above)

1 teaspoon flaky sea salt such as Maldon

12 to 14 very thin slices jalapeño pepper

1. Place two serving plates in the refrigerator to chill.

2. Make the chive oil: In a small saucepan over medium heat, gently heat the oil and chives to 140°F. Pour into a blender and blend for 30 seconds or until smooth. Strain through a paper towel–lined strainer. Let cool.

3. Cut the top and bottom off the blood orange. Then remove the peel, making sure to cut away all the bitter white pith. Segment the fruit over a bowl to collect all the juice, trying not to get any pith or membrane, then squeeze the remaining skeleton to extract all the remaining juice.

4. Remove the side muscle (aka "foot") from the scallops, then slice each one horizontally into quarters.

5. Lay the scallops and blood orange segments on the chilled plates. Add the juice and garnish with the chive oil, flaky salt, and jalapeño slices.

Hokkaido sea scallops are from Japan. It's a sushi-grade scallop known for its sweetness. If you can't find it, you can use a dry diver scallop. No matter what type you use, keep in mind that freshness is key for a crudo recipe. Frozen scallops are usually fresher. This recipe makes more chive oil than you will need. Use it for pastas, beef carpaccio, or vinaigrettes. It will keep for up to 1 week in the refrigerator.

KING CRAB *with* CLARIFIED CHILI-GARLIC BUTTER

YIELD: 2 TO 4 SERVINGS · PREP TIME: 4 MINUTES · COOK TIME: 12 MINUTES

When you need to get back in your partner's good graces, there is no better solution than king crab. Yes, it's expensive, but your partner is worth it. Especially when you need to make something up to them. Katherine can vouch for this.

CLARIFIED BUTTER:

½ cup (1 stick) unsalted butter

6 cloves garlic, sliced

1 pencil chili or bird's-eye chili, sliced

1 shallot, sliced

½ teaspoon kosher salt

½ teaspoon ground black pepper

1 teaspoon chopped fresh parsley, for garnish

1 pound king crab legs, thawed

1. In a small saucepan over low heat, melt the butter with the garlic, chili pepper, and shallot.

2. Continue to slowly heat the butter, periodically skimming the milk solids from the top. When the milk solids start to toast on the bottom of the pan, kill the heat and season the butter with the salt and pepper.

3. In a stockpot, bring ½ inch of water to a boil. Place the crab legs in the pot, cover with a lid, and steam for 8 minutes.

4. Using kitchen scissors, cut both sides of the crab legs to expose the flesh. This makes it dead easy for your partner to enjoy all its goodness. Garnish the clarified butter with the parsley and serve with the crab legs.

You can serve this clarified butter with any shellfish, but it's best with king crab.

When it comes to the heat, we prefer to use a pencil chili pepper. It's milder and easier to work with than most, and it gives the perfect bite of pepper.

SPAGHETTI CARBONARA

YIELD: 2 SERVINGS · PREP TIME: 7 MINUTES · COOK TIME: 12 MINUTES

Like most relationships, carbonara is hard to master unless you put in the work. But when you do, it's a dish that you'll crave on repeat because with pork fat, cheese, and eggs, what's not to love?

7 ounces spaghetti

1½ cups guanciale lardons

1 cup grated pecorino

1½ cups grated Parmigiano-Reggiano cheese

4 large egg yolks

1 teaspoon ground black pepper

1. Bring a large pot of salted water to a boil, then drop in the spaghetti and cook according to the package directions until it reaches the desired doneness. Before draining, reserve about 2 cups of the pasta cooking water.

2. Starting in a cold frying pan, render the fat from the guanciale over medium heat. Continue cooking until the lardons are crispy.

3. Put three-quarters of the cheese in a mixing bowl and add the egg yolks. Whisk in a small amount of the pasta water and 2 tablespoons of the guanciale fat.

4. Add the spaghetti to the bowl and stir. Adjust the consistency as desired with more pasta water or extra cheese. Toss in half of the guanciale and plate.

5. Garnish with the remaining cheese and guanciale and finish with pepper.

It's always better to have the pasta looser at first, so always add some of the pasta cooking water. The sauce will tighten up and thicken as you enjoy your carbonara.

RANDY BO BANDY
CHEESEBURGER

YIELD: 4 BURGERS • PREP TIME: 10 TO 14 MINUTES, PLUS 1½ HOURS FOR DOUGH TO RISE
COOK TIME: 25 MINUTES

All you need to do to be quickly forgiven is to serve up a burger that's better than takeout. Honestly, it's that simple. Fluffy homemade buns are one of the secrets. The extras can be stored in a freezer-safe bag or container for up to a week.

HAMBURGER BUNS:
(MAKES 8 BUNS)

1 cup warm water

3 tablespoons warm milk

2¼ teaspoons instant yeast

2½ tablespoons granulated sugar

3 cups bread flour

½ cup all-purpose flour

1½ teaspoons fine salt

3 tablespoons unsalted butter, softened

1 large egg, room temperature, lightly beaten, for brushing the dough balls

CHEESEBURGERS:

1½ pounds medium ground beef

1½ teaspoons kosher salt

¾ teaspoon ground black pepper

4 slices American or cheddar cheese

4 Hamburger Buns (from above)

¼ cup (½ stick) unsalted butter

2 tablespoons Dijon mustard

12 slices pickle

4 slices tomato

4 paper-thin slices onion

4 leaf lettuce leaves

1. Make the buns: Combine the warm water and milk in a small bowl, then stir in the yeast and sugar Let sit for 5 minutes. Put the rest of the ingredients, except the egg, in a stand mixer. Slowly add the yeast mixture to the dry ingredients and mix on medium speed until smooth, about 6 minutes. Transfer to a lightly oiled bowl and let double in size, about 1 hour. Punch down and divide into eight equal portions. Form into balls, cover with a kitchen towel, and let rise for another 30 minutes.

2. Preheat the oven to 375°F. Brush the dough balls with the egg wash. Bake for 16 minutes, or until golden.

3. Divide the ground beef into four 6-ounce portions. Gently mold into perfect burger patties about 15 percent wider than your buns. Season with the salt and pepper.

4. Preheat an ungreased grill pan until smoking hot. Sear the patties on the pan without pushing, poking, or touching them. When a crust appears after 2 to 3 minutes, flip them and top with the cheese. Sear in peace for another 2 to 3 minutes to lock in the beautiful juices; do not smash or poke. This cook time will give you medium-done burgers.

5. Meanwhile, split four of the buns, then butter and toast them in a hot frying pan. Dress the buns with the toppings: mustard, pickles, onion, lettuce leaves, and tomato.

6. Remove the cheeseburgers from the heat and place each one on a bottom bun. Crown with the top bun and serve.

When it comes to this burger, seasoning is key. Other key? Keep it juicy by leaving the burgers be when cooking (no smashing), and don't overcook or overdress.

BY YOUR
SIDE

Sides that pair perfectly with
your favorite dishes

CHEDDAR JALAPEÑO
CREAMED CORN

YIELD: 4 SERVINGS · PREP TIME: 10 MINUTES · COOK TIME: 15 MINUTES

Are you firing up the grill to make your special someone a perfectly cooked steak? Well, may we suggest pairing it with this classic steakhouse side? Adding both regular and smoked cheddar and jalapeño to creamed corn will give you extra points for the flavor complexity. It'll give your date that steakhouse experience without breaking the bank. Plus, it's even better because it's made by you.

6 ears corn, shucked

2 cloves garlic, sliced

1 shallot, finely diced

1 jalapeño pepper, finely diced

1½ tablespoons unsalted butter

1 tablespoon all-purpose flour

½ cup dry white wine

½ cup heavy cream

¼ cup shredded cheddar cheese

¼ cup shredded smoked cheddar cheese

1 teaspoon kosher salt

½ teaspoon ground black pepper

Sprig of fresh cilantro, for garnish

1. Cut the kernels off the ears of corn, then scrape the cobs over a bowl with the flat edge of a knife to get all the pulp and "milk."

2. In a large frying pan, sauté the garlic, shallot, and jalapeño in the butter over medium-low heat. When soft, add the flour and toast gently while stirring for 3 to 4 minutes, until it turns a light blonde color.

3. Deglaze with the wine and continue cooking until reduced by half, then add the cream and reduce by one-quarter.

4. Toss in the corn and corn milk and simmer, uncovered, until the sauce gently coats the back of a spoon and the corn is tender but still pops, about 6 minutes.

5. Stir in the cheddar and allow to melt. Then season with the salt and pepper. Garnish with the sprig of cilantro and serve.

LOVE TAP If you're in a pinch and need a side on the fly, you can use frozen corn for this recipe. But this shortcut will get you an 8 out of 10 instead of a 10 out of 10.

CHARRED
ZUCCHINI ROMESCO

YIELD: 2 SERVINGS · PREP TIME: 6 MINUTES · COOK TIME: 8 MINUTES

When it comes to vegetable sides, zucchini is always the one that Randy wants, especially if it's grilled and paired with a tasty romesco sauce. This is served at room temperature or barely warm, so it can take a seat back for a bit, freeing you up to focus all of your attention on your date.

CHARRED ZUCCHINI:

4 medium zucchini

½ teaspoon kosher salt

2 tablespoons extra-virgin olive oil

½ teaspoon ground black pepper

ROMESCO SAUCE:

2 medium red bell peppers

2 tablespoons sun-dried tomatoes (packed in oil)

2 cloves garlic, peeled

½ cup raw almonds, toasted

2 tablespoons red wine vinegar

2 tablespoons extra-virgin olive oil

1 teaspoon chili powder

1 teaspoon smoked paprika

1 teaspoon kosher salt

½ teaspoon ground black pepper

FOR GARNISH:

4 ounces fresh mozzarella di bufala, torn into 1-inch pieces

2 tablespoons small fresh mint leaves

1 tablespoon extra-virgin olive oil

½ teaspoon ground black pepper

1. Halve the zucchini lengthwise, then score the cut sides in a crisscross pattern. (This will help them cook evenly.) Season with the salt and set aside for about 4 minutes, then pat dry.

2. Meanwhile, preheat a large cast-iron frying pan over medium heat. When hot, pour in the olive oil and place the zucchini cut side down in the pan. Sear for a few minutes, until golden brown, then flip and cook the other side for about 1½ minutes (the skin side should be more lightly cooked). The zucchini should be charred on the outside and tender but still firm to the bite on the inside; if not, cook it a bit longer. Remove to a cutting board and slice on the diagonal into 2- to 3-inch sections.

3. Make the romesco sauce: Using tongs, char the peppers over a gas burner until the skin is blackened. If you don't have a gas stovetop, you can use a BBQ grill, grill pan, or kitchen torch. Immediately place the charred peppers in a bowl and seal with plastic wrap; the steam created by the peppers helps the skins release more easily. Let rest for 10 minutes, then scrape off the skins with a knife. Remove the core and seeds from the peppers and place the flesh in a blender with the remaining romesco ingredients. Blend until silky smooth.

4. Evenly cover two serving plates with the romesco sauce, then top with the zucchini pieces. Garnish with the mozzarella, mint, olive oil, and pepper.

Fresh mozzarella di bufala—mozzarella made from the milk of water buffaloes—takes this dish to the next level. But if you can't find it, regular cow's milk mozzarella will work. For the mint leaves, use the small leaves found at the top of the sprigs that often form in clusters.

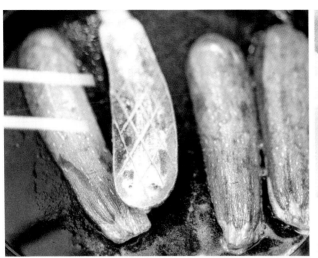

RAPINI *and* LEEK *with* CANNELLINI BEANS

YIELD: 2 TO 4 SERVINGS · PREP TIME: 8 MINUTES · COOK TIME: 14 MINUTES

People tend to give rapini (aka broccoli rabe) the side eye because of its bitter flavor, but it's so underrated. We all need to embrace the bitterness sometimes. So take its side and pair it with leeks and cannellini beans. Warning: This dish is so good that you may move it up the roster and make it the main course.

2 tablespoons extra-virgin olive oil

1 tablespoon unsalted butter

6 cloves garlic, sliced

2 red chilies, such as pepperoncini, sliced

1 large leek, washed and chopped

1 bunch rapini, washed and chopped

½ cup dry white wine

1 (15.5-ounce) can cannellini beans, drained and rinsed

½ teaspoon kosher salt

¼ teaspoon ground black pepper

3 tablespoons grated Parmigiano-Reggiano cheese

¼ cup fresh basil leaves

2 slices bread, grilled, for serving (optional)

1. In a large frying pan over medium heat, gently heat the olive oil and butter. Sweat the garlic and chilies in the fat just until they are softened.

2. Toss in the leek and rapini and cook, stirring from time to time, until you see hints of color. Deglaze with the wine and add the beans. Cover the pan and turn down the heat to low; allow to steam until the rapini is tender, 8 to 9 minutes.

3. Season with the salt and pepper and finish with the Parmigiano-Reggiano and basil. Serve with grilled bread or straight up.

Be sure to wash the leek well. Leeks are dirty girls! Begin by cutting off the dark green top (reserve it for stock). You will use only the white part for this recipe. Trim the root end at the bottom, then cut the leek in half lengthwise. Peel back each layer and wash in between, then pat dry.

TURMERIC
MAPLE SYRUP
ROASTED CARROTS

YIELD: 4 TO 6 SERVINGS · PREP TIME: 12 MINUTES · COOK TIME: 24 MINUTES

If you carrot about your love at all (pun intended!), you're going to want to pair your favorite entrées with this vibrant side. After all, she or he deserves the best, and that's what these roasted carrots will deliver.

2 pounds medium heirloom carrots, preferably multicolored

¼ cup (½ stick) unsalted butter

¼ cup maple syrup

1 tablespoon fresh lemon juice, plus extra if needed

1½ teaspoons grainy Dijon mustard

1½ teaspoons grated garlic

1½ teaspoons grated turmeric root

1 teaspoon kosher salt

½ teaspoon ground black pepper

1. Preheat the oven to 450°F, using the convection setting. If your oven doesn't have a convection setting, preheat it to 475°F. Line a sheet pan with parchment paper.

2. Wash and dry the carrots thoroughly.

3. Make the glaze: Melt the butter in a small saucepan over medium-low heat, then stir in the maple syrup, lemon juice, Dijon, garlic, turmeric, salt, and pepper. Slide the pan off the heat and taste to check the balance of flavors, adjusting it if needed (see Love Tap).

4. Set the carrots on the prepared sheet pan and toss with the glaze, coating the carrots on all sides.

5. Roast for 12 minutes and toss again, then continue to roast until golden and fork-tender, another 6 to 10 minutes.

This simple dish is all about balancing sweetness and acidity and then letting the oven do the rest. Some lemons are more acidic than others, so make sure you taste the glaze before it goes into the oven; it should be slightly tart, because the carrots will provide a lot of sweetness as they roast. Add a touch more lemon juice if needed. Using fresh turmeric gives the dish a uniquely vibrant, citrusy, and spicy flavor.

ASPARAGUS SALAD *with* WHIPPED GOAT CHEESE *and* HARISSA HAZELNUTS

YIELD: 4 SERVINGS · PREP TIME: 6 MINUTES · COOK TIME: 8 MINUTES

Whip your side game into shape with this salad that features asparagus prepared two ways: roasted and raw, cut into thin, elegant ribbons. The crunchiness of the fresh asparagus ribbons and toasted hazelnuts contrasted with the tender roasted asparagus and ultra-smooth texture of the whipped goat cheese will have your partner asking for seconds. So make sure you make extra, because it's just that good.

WHIPPED GOAT CHEESE:

5 ounces fresh (soft) goat cheese

¼ cup plus 2 tablespoons dry white wine

2 tablespoons honey

1 tablespoon fresh lemon juice

ASPARAGUS:

1 bunch thick asparagus

2 tablespoons extra-virgin olive oil, divided

1 teaspoon kosher salt, divided

1 teaspoon ground black pepper, divided

1 tablespoon fresh lemon juice

HARISSA HAZELNUTS:

1 teaspoon harissa

1 teaspoon extra-virgin olive oil

3 tablespoons hazelnuts

We find that the perfect way to cook asparagus is in the oven or on the grill. Just make sure you don't overcook it.

1. Put the goat cheese in a medium mixing bowl. Add the wine, honey, and lemon juice and whip with a whisk until the ingredients are combined and the texture is smooth. Set aside.

2. Preheat the oven to 450°F.

3. Chop the bottoms off the asparagus, then separate the spears into two equal portions. Toss one portion with 1 tablespoon of the olive oil and ½ teaspoon each of the salt and pepper. Place on a sheet pan and roast until tender, about 6 minutes.

4. Meanwhile, peel the remaining asparagus into ribbons and dress with the lemon juice and remaining tablespoon of olive oil, then season with the remaining ½ teaspoon of salt and ½ teaspoon of pepper.

5. Make the harissa hazelnuts: In a small frying pan, lightly toast the harissa in the olive oil over medium heat, shaking the pan often. Toss in the hazelnuts and continue to shake the pan until the nuts are toasted and fully covered in the harissa. Remove and chop.

6. Spread a quarter of the whipped goat cheese mixture on a serving plate and top with a quarter of the roasted asparagus, shaved asparagus, and harissa toasted hazelnuts. Repeat to make a total of four servings

IRISH BROWN SODA BREAD

YIELD: 1 LOAF (4 TO 6 SERVINGS) · PREP TIME: 12 MINUTES · COOK TIME: 55 MINUTES

Randy worked at a restaurant in Ireland for a year, and he baked this Irish soda bread daily. Made with wholesome grains and seeds, it is very different from the refined white flour version made with currants and caraway seeds. It was inspired by Randy's head chef at the time, Niall Hill. They make it every year for St. Patrick's Day to celebrate the love of the Irish and their love for this bread.

1½ teaspoons bacon fat or butter, for the pan

400 grams coarse whole-wheat flour (aka wholemeal flour)

100 grams bread flour

50 grams rolled oats, plus extra for the pan

50 grams pumpkin seeds

50 grams raw sunflower seeds

1 teaspoon baking soda

1 teaspoon kosher salt

1 tablespoon fancy molasses

1⅔ cups buttermilk

1 large egg, beaten

2 tablespoons extra-virgin olive oil

1. Preheat the oven to 400°F, using the convection setting. If your oven doesn't have a convection setting, preheat it to 425°F. Place a small pot of water in the oven.

2. Grease a 5 by 9-inch loaf pan with the bacon fat and dust with oats.

3. In a large mixing bowl, whisk together all the dry ingredients and make a well in the center.

4. In a separate bowl, mix together all the wet ingredients and pour them into the well in the dry ingredients.

5. Stir the wet and dry ingredients together just until combined, then knead the mixture in the bowl until you have a wet dough, about 7 minutes.

6. Form the dough into a loaf shape and place in the prepared pan. Bake for 45 to 55 minutes, until the top is golden and a toothpick inserted in the center of the loaf comes out clean.

7. Remove from the oven and let rest on a wire rack for 20 minutes before slicing.

LOVE TIP: Making bread from scratch can be intimidating, but that's not the case with this recipe. It uses baking soda instead of yeast, so it's a great option for beginners. Just be sure to weigh your dry ingredients for best results. The bread will keep for up to 6 days, or you can preslice it and freeze the slices.

POTATO COLCANNON

YIELD: 6 TO 8 SERVINGS · PREP TIME: 14 MINUTES · COOK TIME: 22 MINUTES

When Randy was a young cook, he decided to go to Ireland for a year. He quickly understood the Irish love of potatoes, butter, and cream. So when he came back to Canada, he brought this love back with him, and potatoes have become one of our favorite side dishes to enjoy together. We always look for a good main dish to pair them with because there is just no better side. Make these potatoes and you'll understand why.

2½ pounds Yukon Gold potatoes, peeled

1½ teaspoons kosher salt

¼ head savoy cabbage, thinly sliced

3 cloves garlic, sliced

1 tablespoon fresh thyme leaves

½ cup (1 stick) plus 1 tablespoon unsalted butter, plus extra for garnish

¼ cup dry white wine

¼ cup milk

½ cup heavy cream

⅛ teaspoon ground white pepper

½ cup thinly sliced green onions, divided

1. Leave smaller potatoes whole and cut larger ones in half or in quarters to match the size of smallest ones so that the potatoes cook evenly.

2. Put the potatoes in a large pot and cover with cold water. Add the salt and bring to a simmer over medium heat. Continue to simmer until the potatoes are tender, 15 to 20 minutes. Meanwhile, cook the cabbage.

3. In a large frying pan over medium heat, sauté the cabbage with the garlic and thyme in 1 tablespoon of the butter. When the cabbage and garlic start to color, deglaze the pan with the wine and cover with a lid. Steam until tender, then set aside.

4. When the potatoes are tender, drain them, then return them to the pot to dry, using the residual heat of the pot. (If, after a minute or so, there is some water remaining, turn the heat under the pot to low until the water evaporates.) Turn the heat back on to medium and add the milk, cream, remaining ½ cup of butter, and white pepper.

5. Using a potato masher, mash as hard as possible until the potatoes are smooth. Add the cabbage and three-quarters of the green onions and stir to combine.

6. Adjust the seasoning and plate, then garnish with the remaining green onions and a thick pat of butter.

LOVE TAP   Drying out the boiled potatoes is a must. You need to get the water out to make room for the milk, cream, and butter.

ONE-PAN
SMASHED POTATOES

YIELD: 2 TO 4 SERVINGS · PREP TIME: 6 MINUTES · COOK TIME: 25 MINUTES

This is one of our favorite sides to pair with almost everything we cook, and it's soon to be your go-to side, too. Our video for these delicious one-pan potatoes went viral, and our followers continue to ask for the recipe. Because it's all done in one pan, the prep and cleanup are just too easy. So curl up your main course next to these smashed baby potatoes and enjoy a decadent date night.

1 pound baby Yukon Gold potatoes, rinsed

¼ cup extra-virgin olive oil

2 tablespoons unsalted butter

4 cloves garlic, halved

1 shallot, sliced

2 tablespoons capers (optional)

1 sprig fresh rosemary

½ teaspoon kosher salt

FOR GARNISH:

1 tablespoon fresh lemon juice

1 teaspoon flaky sea salt

¼ teaspoon ground black pepper

Thinly sliced fresh chives

1. Place the potatoes in a large frying pan and pour in water to barely cover the potatoes. Do not overcrowd the pan. If needed, boil the potatoes in batches.

2. Add the olive oil, butter, garlic, shallot, capers (if using), rosemary, and salt. Bring to a lively simmer over medium heat and let cook until the potatoes are tender and nearly all the water has evaporated, about 20 minutes. At this point, the potatoes will be starting to caramelize.

3. Smash the potatoes lightly with a ramekin (just enough to flatten the top and bottom) and continue to caramelize, flipping them over once or twice.

4. When the potatoes have a very crispy exterior, garnish with the lemon juice, flaky salt, pepper, and chives and serve.

This recipe is a simple lesson in building flavor and texture through evaporation and caramelization. We are always asked if stock can be used instead of water. Short answer is yes, but if you do that, omit the kosher salt. We prefer using water because we want the potatoes to take on the other flavors we've added. The stock, however, will intensify the color of the caramelization.

CREAMY PEPPERCORN SAUCE

YIELD: ½ CUP (2 SERVINGS) · PREP TIME: 6 MINUTES · COOK TIME: 12 MINUTES

This sassy sauce is packed with shallot, garlic, butter, brandy, stock, and cream, and it's so yummy that we think it deserves to be elevated to side dish status. Pair it with your favorite cut of steak (or other favorite protein) and dip into it with your partner. Warning: You just might find that you'll need more sauce and less protein.

2 tablespoons unsalted butter

1 shallot, finely diced

1 clove garlic, finely diced

3 ounces brandy, preferably Armagnac

¾ cup beef stock

¼ cup plus 2 tablespoons heavy cream

2 teaspoons cracked black peppercorns

1. Melt the butter in a medium heavy-bottomed frying pan over medium heat, then add the shallot and garlic and sauté until translucent. Deglaze the pan with the brandy and let the alcohol burn off, reducing by half.

2. Pour in the beef stock and reduce by half again. Then add the cream and pepper and reduce by half, or until you see very large bubbles forming.

3. Remove and serve.

This is a perfect sauce. It can be made days ahead of time and reheated when needed, so you can use it for multiple recipes.

HAPPY
ENDINGS

Delectable dessert recipes to ensure
all your dates have a happy ending

VANILLA BEAN
SOFT-SERVE

YIELD: 2 TO 4 SERVINGS · PREP TIME: 12 MINUTES, PLUS 2 HOURS TO CHILL BASE
AND 25 MINUTES TO CHURN · COOK TIME: 5 MINUTES

When it comes to ice cream, sure, you can take the easy way out and just go out for some. But why not elevate your ice cream dates and make it at home? It's 1,000 times fresher, better, and more romantic when you make it yourself because it's full of love. So treat yourselves to this homemade vanilla bean soft-serve. We guarantee you'll both be happier.

1½ cups heavy cream

1½ cups whole milk

1 vanilla bean (about 6 inches long), split

3 large egg yolks

¾ cup granulated sugar

½ teaspoon kosher salt

½ to 1 cup fresh mandarin orange juice (optional)

SPECIAL EQUIPMENT:

Ice cream maker

1. Pour the cream and milk into a medium saucepan. Scrape the seeds from the vanilla pod and add the seeds and pod to the pan. Bring the mixture to a gentle simmer over medium heat.

2. In a medium bowl, mix the egg yolks, sugar, and salt until combined.

3. Pluck the vanilla pod out of the cream mixture, then very slowly whisk the hot dairy into the egg yolk mixture. Once all the dairy is incorporated, place the bowl in an ice bath to cool, then chill the base for at least 2 hours.

4. Churn in an ice cream maker until it gets to soft-serve consistency, about 25 minutes, depending on your machine.

5. Once at soft-serve consistency, scoop the ice cream into a piping bag and pipe out a portion into a cocktail glass. Serve straight up or floating in ¼ cup of mandarin orange juice, if desired.

It's all about the vanilla bean. Yes, vanilla beans are pricey, but you need the pod for that delicious vanilla flavor that surpasses any extract.

Does your date like orange Creamsicles? Then be sure to pour some mandarin orange juice into the cocktail glass before piping in the soft-serve. It's a top-shelf version that is sure to impress.

Leftover ice cream will keep for up to a month; once frozen, it will lose its soft-serve texture. Let set on the counter for 12 minutes before serving.

BRÛLÉED FIGS
with SABAYON

YIELD: 2 TO 4 SERVINGS · PREP TIME: 10 MINUTES · COOK TIME: 8 MINUTES

Did you forget dessert? No problem! Whip up some sabayon sauce and serve it with brûléed figs. (Sabayon is simply frothed egg yolks, sugar, and sweet wine gently cooked over a water bath.) This is the easiest dessert to make in a pinch because it takes almost no time, and it'll definitely put a smile on your partner's face.

6 fresh figs, halved

3 tablespoons granulated sugar, divided

4 large egg yolks

¼ teaspoon kosher salt

¼ cup Marsala wine, divided

½ teaspoon fresh lemon juice

¼ cup macadamia nuts, chopped, for garnish

SPECIAL EQUIPMENT:

Kitchen torch

1. Lightly sprinkle the figs with 1 tablespoon of the sugar and blowtorch them on the flesh side until golden. Cut into quarters and stand them up in a large serving bowl with shallow sides.

2. Make the sabayon: In the top of a double boiler, or in a heatproof bowl that fits snugly in a saucepan, whisk the egg yolks, remaining 2 tablespoons of sugar, salt, and a splash of the wine until the mixture is frothy. Place over a simmering water bath and whisk aggressively until the sauce has doubled in volume, about 6 minutes. While continuing to whisk, add the remaining wine and the lemon juice. Continue whisking until it reaches ribbon stage (you'll know it's at ribbon stage when you lift the whisk and you get a long, steady flow that holds its shape and falls back into the bowl like a ribbon). This will take some effort, but you will be rewarded.

3. The flavor of the finished sauce should be sweet, boozy, and velvety. Taste and add a drop more lemon juice if needed, or, if you don't find the sauce sweet enough, a drop of wine.

4. To serve, pour the warm sauce in between the figs. Torch the figs one more time, garnish with the macadamia nuts, and serve.

Fresh figs have a short season. Don't let that stop you from trying this recipe. Other soft seasonal fruits can be used at other times of the year: peaches, nectarines, and plums would be good options.

BURNT CHEESECAKE

YIELD: 10 SERVINGS · PREP TIME: 15 MINUTES, PLUS 3 HOURS TO CHILL · COOK TIME: 1 HOUR

We first fell in love with this style of cheesecake, with its burnt top and super creamy interior, on our honeymoon in Spain. We knew we had to bring it back to our kitchen and put our own spin on it. So whenever we want to reminisce about our honeymoon, we make this cheesecake, and it instantly takes us back. There's no better happy ending than that.

4 (8-ounce) packages cream cheese, softened

1⅓ cups granulated sugar

5 large eggs, room temperature

1¼ cups heavy cream, room temperature

1 vanilla bean (about 6 inches long), split and seeds scraped

3 tablespoons brandy

1 teaspoon kosher salt

¼ cup bread flour, sifted

SPECIAL EQUIPMENT:

9-inch springform pan

1. Preheat the oven to 425°F and line the bottom and sides of the springform pan with parchment paper.

2. Toss the cream cheese and sugar into a stand mixer and whisk at medium speed for 3 minutes, or until the sugar has dissolved and the texture is smooth.

3. Add one egg at a time, wiping down the sides of the bowl as you go. Turn the mixer down to low speed and add the cream, vanilla seeds, brandy, and salt. When mixed in, slowly incorporate the flour.

4. Pour the batter into the prepared pan and bake for 1 hour, or until the top is darkly caramelized. The cake will still be jiggly all the way from the center to the edges. This is as it should be. You want it undercooked more than slightly.

5. Remove from the oven and let rest for a minimum of 3 hours. Then remove from the pan, slice, and serve at room temperature.

LOVE TAP Don't be afraid to underbake this cake. You want it to have some jiggle, jiggle. If you're lucky enough to have leftovers, they can be stored in the fridge for up to 1 week.

OLIVE OIL
CHOCOLATE TART

YIELD: 12 TO 16 SERVINGS · PREP TIME: 12 MINUTES, PLUS 2 HOURS TO CHILL DOUGH AND TART
COOK TIME: 10 MINUTES

When it comes to dessert, chocolate is just about everyone's love language. This decadent tart is no exception. It's been on our restaurant menu at The Farmhouse since the beginning. Whether it's your first date, your anniversary, or just a night in together, this recipe will have you falling in love all over again.

SHORT PASTRY:

2¼ cups all-purpose flour

¾ cup (1½ sticks) cold unsalted butter, grated using the medium holes on a box grater

½ teaspoon kosher salt

6 tablespoons ice water, divided

CHOCOLATE FILLING:

2½ cups heavy cream

3 tablespoons extra-virgin olive oil

3 tablespoons maple syrup

2½ cups dark chocolate chips (about 53% cacao)

1 tablespoon flaky sea salt, for garnish

SPECIAL EQUIPMENT:

12-inch tart pan with removable bottom

Pie weights (optional)

1. Make the short pastry: Toss the flour, butter, and salt into a food processor with 3 tablespoons of the ice water. Blitz until the mixture is crumbly with some pea-sized pebbles of butter, then slowly add the rest of the water with the machine running. When it comes together into a workable dough, remove and form into a large disk shape, about 6 inches in diameter. (You will know the dough is workable if it holds together when pinched between your thumb and finger. If it does not, add a teaspoon of water.) Wrap in plastic wrap and chill for 30 minutes.

2. Preheat the oven to 350°F. Have on hand a 12-inch tart pan with a removable bottom and pie weights. If you don't have pie weights, dried chickpeas or other beans will work just as well. Cut a circle of parchment the same diameter as the tart pan.

3. Remove the dough from the plastic wrap and roll it out between two sheets of parchment paper into a 14- to 15-inch circle. Place in the tart pan, pressing it into the corners and trimming excess from the top. Place the parchment circle on top of the dough and add two layers of pie weights. This is referred to as blind baking. Blind-bake until the dough is light blonde, 9 to 10 minutes.

4. Remove from the oven, let cool, and remove the pie weights.

5. Make the chocolate filling: In a medium saucepan over medium heat, bring the cream, olive oil, and maple syrup to a very gentle simmer. Turn off the heat and add the chocolate chips. Stir fairly aggressively until the chocolate is completely melted and the mixture is smooth. Pour the molten chocolate into the tart shell and chill for 1½ hours.

6. Garnish with the flaky salt and cut into servings of your desired size, keeping in mind that this is a very decadent dessert.

Since chocolate is the key ingredient in this dessert, buy the best-quality chocolate that you can find for the best-tasting results (such as Callebaut, Lindt, or Valrhona). Don't be afraid of the quantity of finishing salt used; it needs an aggressive garnish of flaky salt to bring out its full flavor. This can be stored in the refrigerator for up to 1 week—if you're lucky enough to have any that long.

COCONUT
CREAM PIE

YIELD: 6 TO 8 SERVINGS · PREP TIME: 7 MINUTES, PLUS 4 HOURS TO CHILL · COOK TIME: 12 MINUTES

As you know, we met at Randy's old restaurant, Oscar's. To this day, twenty-five years later, this pie is still on the menu there. So that in itself should tell you that this dessert stands the test of time, just like a solid relationship. But every long-haul relationship needs a surprise from time to time, like here with a shaved white chocolate garnish. The addition of white chocolate gives the pie extra flavor and butteriness that we all crave. Now that's a happy ending in our eyes.

GRAHAM CRACKER CRUST:

1 sleeve graham crackers

¼ cup granulated sugar

6 tablespoons (¾ stick) unsalted butter, melted

¼ cup sweetened coconut flakes

½ teaspoon kosher salt

FILLING:

3 cups half-and-half

2 large eggs

¾ cup granulated sugar

½ cup all-purpose flour

⅓ cup cornstarch

¼ teaspoon kosher salt

1 cup sweetened coconut flakes, toasted, divided

¼ cup coconut milk

1 teaspoon vanilla extract

TOPPING:

1¼ cups heavy cream

2 tablespoons instant vanilla pudding mix

¼ cup granulated sugar

½ teaspoon vanilla extract

Toasted coconut flakes (from above)

2 tablespoons shaved white chocolate (optional)

1. Preheat the oven to 350°F. Have on hand a 9-inch pie pan.

2. Make the crust: Pulse the graham crackers and sugar in a food processor or blender until finely ground. Add the butter, coconut flakes, and salt and blend until well combined. Transfer to the pie pan and, using the bottom of a glass or measuring cup, evenly pack the crust into the bottom and up the sides of the pan. It should be about ¼ inch thick.

3. Bake for 8 to 10 minutes, until set and starting to color. When done, remove from the oven and set aside to cool.

4. Meanwhile, make the filling: In a large saucepan over medium heat, gently stir the half-and-half with the eggs, sugar, flour, cornstarch, and salt until combined. Add 90 percent of the toasted coconut flakes and continue stirring. When the custard starts to thicken, remove the pan from the heat and pour in the coconut milk and vanilla. Bring to a soft simmer over medium heat and cook, stirring constantly, until the custard is thick and coats the back of a spoon, 8 to 10 minutes. When the filling has thickened to a pudding-like consistency, pour into the pie crust. Let cool, then chill for 4 hours.

5. Make the whipped cream topping: Whip the heavy cream with the instant pudding mix, sugar, and vanilla until firm peaks form. Layer evenly onto the pie and garnish with the reserved toasted coconut flakes and white chocolate shavings, if desired, just before serving.

6. Slice and serve.

The instant pudding mix is a pastry chef's hairspray. It will keep your whipped cream stiff and peaked for days. Leftovers can be stored in the fridge for up to a week.

RASPBERRY CREAM CHEESE COBBLER

YIELD: 2 TO 4 SERVINGS · PREP TIME: 8 MINUTES · COOK TIME: 25 MINUTES

Randy isn't a big dessert guy, but when he created this cobbler, we were both blown away by the amazing flavor of this simple dessert. It's what you would call a cook's dessert because all you do is assemble it and fire it in the oven. Great results with minimal effort so you can spend more time enjoying time with your partner on date night instead of working away in the kitchen.

3 tablespoons melted unsalted butter, for the pan

BATTER:

½ cup granulated sugar

½ cup all-purpose flour

1 teaspoon baking powder

½ cup 2% milk

½ teaspoon fresh lemon juice

12 ounces raspberries

1 tablespoon granulated sugar

1 teaspoon ground cinnamon

1 teaspoon vanilla extract

6 ounces (¾ cup) cream cheese, cut into ½- to 1-inch chunks

FOR SERVING/GARNISH:

Vanilla ice cream (see page 228)

Flaky sea salt

1. Preheat the oven to 400°F.

2. Pour the melted butter into an 8-inch oven-safe frying pan and tilt to evenly coat the bottom and sides.

3. Make the batter: In a mixing bowl, whisk together the sugar, flour, baking powder, milk, and lemon juice until smooth. Pour the batter into the prepared pan.

4. In another bowl, toss the raspberries in the sugar, cinnamon, and vanilla, giving them a shake to evenly coat.

5. Gently layer the berries over the batter and top with the cream cheese chunks.

6. Bake for 25 minutes, or until golden brown.

7. Let cool slightly, then serve with a scoop of vanilla ice cream and a sprinkle of flaky salt.

This cobbler does best baked at a high temp. You need that wet batter to cook through, and you want a nice caramelized top on it. If you don't have an 8-inch oven-safe frying pan, you can use an 8-inch cake pan instead.

CHOCOLATE MAPLE BROWN BUTTER COOKIES

YIELD: 9 LARGE COOKIES · PREP TIME: 12 MINUTES, PLUS 30 MINUTES TO CHILL BUTTER AND DOUGH
COOK TIME: 43 MINUTES

Guarantee a happy ending on your next date night with these gourmet cookies.
They are gooey on the inside and salty on the outside. Let's just say this is one
cookie that you and your partner will keep coming back to.

½ cup (1 stick) plus 1 tablespoon unsalted butter

125 grams dark brown sugar

60 grams maple syrup

1 large egg

½ teaspoon vanilla extract

150 grams all-purpose flour

¼ teaspoon baking soda

¼ teaspoon baking powder

½ teaspoon kosher salt

6 ounces semisweet chocolate chips (about 42% cacao)

6 ounces dark chocolate chunks (about 54% cacao)

2 teaspoons flaky sea salt, for garnish

1. In a small saucepan over medium heat, melt the butter until the milk solids caramelize on the bottom of the pan, about 4 minutes. You want the milk solids to be a chestnut brown color. Pour the brown butter into a heatproof bowl and place in the refrigerator for about 15 minutes, until cool.

2. In a stand mixer fitted with the paddle attachment, or using a medium mixing bowl and an electric hand mixer, cream the cooled brown butter with the brown sugar and maple syrup on medium-high speed. Keep beating until the sugar is dissolved and the mixture is creamy.

3. Add the egg and vanilla and mix to combine, then turn down the speed to medium and slowly mix in the flour, baking soda, and baking powder until combined.

4. Fold in three-quarters of the chocolate by hand. Chill the dough for 15 minutes.

5. Preheat the oven to 350°F and line a baking sheet with parchment paper.

6. Divide the dough into 9 equal portions, form each into a ball, and place on the prepared baking sheet, leaving 2 inches of space between them. Pat down the balls with your hand to a 1-inch thickness and top with the remaining chocolate.

7. Bake until the edges are crispy, 11 to 13 minutes. Transfer to a wire rack, garnish with the flaky salt, and let cool before enjoying.

LOVE TAP

When we say brown butter, we mean it. Don't be afraid to really toast the milk solids. It will give the cookies a deep toffee taste that is hard to describe.

STICKY TOFFEE
PUDDING

YIELD: 4 SERVINGS · PREP TIME: 10 MINUTES · COOK TIME: 1 HOUR

We all know that happy endings can get a little sticky, so why not embrace it?
Whip up a classic sticky toffee pudding, but make it on the healthy side by
throwing in some date for the perfect date. See what we did there?

CARAMEL SAUCE:

2½ cups heavy cream, divided

½ cup (1 stick) unsalted butter

1 cup granulated sugar

½ cup maple syrup

DATE CAKE:

6 ounces pitted dates

½ cup water

¼ cup (½ stick) unsalted butter, softened

¾ cup packed dark brown sugar

1 large egg

¾ cup plus 1 tablespoon all-purpose flour

1 teaspoon baking powder

¼ teaspoon baking soda

1 teaspoon kosher salt

½ teaspoon vanilla extract

FOR SERVING/GARNISH:

Vanilla ice cream (see page 228)

Fresh mint leaves (optional)

1. Make the sauce: Pour 1¼ cups of the cream into a medium saucepan and add the butter, sugar, and maple syrup. Bring to a simmer over medium heat, whisking every 30 seconds. Continue to simmer gently for 30 to 40 minutes, whisking for 30 seconds every 5 minutes, until golden to amber in color, depending on your preference. When it gets to your desired darkness, slowly whisk in the remaining 1¼ cups of cream to stop the cooking, then strain and set aside. Meanwhile, begin making the cake.

2. Preheat the oven to 350°F. Have on hand four 4-ounce ramekins and a 3-inch-deep baking dish or pan for a 1-inch water bath.

3. In a small saucepan over medium heat, simmer the dates in the water until the dates are soft and the water has reduced by one-third to one-half, 12 minutes or so. Blend the softened dates with the cooking liquid to make a puree; set aside.

4. In a stand mixer fitted with the paddle attachment, or using a medium mixing bowl and an electric hand mixer, mix the butter, brown sugar, and egg on medium speed until creamy. Add the date puree and the remaining ingredients.

5. Divide the batter evenly among the ramekins, filling them to the rim, and place in the baking dish. Pour hot water into the dish until it comes 1 inch up the sides of the ramekins. Place the dish with the ramekins in the oven and bake for 20 to 25 minutes, until the puddings have risen about ¼ inch and have a slight jiggle. Do not overcook.

6. Remove and let cool for 10 minutes. Turn out onto a plate, cover with the caramel sauce, and top with a scoop of vanilla ice cream. Garnish with fresh mint, if desired.

Freeze leftover cakes and, when you need an ace up your sleeve, place back in the ramekins and steam for 6 minutes. Never have an unhappy ending again!

MERINGUE *with* LEMON CURD

YIELD: 6 SERVINGS · PREP TIME: 20 MINUTES, PLUS 2 HOURS TO REST IN OVEN
COOK TIME: 1 HOUR 15 MINUTES

This recipe is a perfect example of putting the work in early and benefiting later, when it comes together quickly and easily. Both the meringue and the curd can be made up to a week in advance; store the meringue in an airtight container on the counter and the curd in the fridge. This dessert guarantees a happy ending because you can eat it right away or enjoy the lemon curd in the morning on toast after a perfect date night.

MERINGUE:

4 large egg whites, room temperature

1 cup superfine sugar, divided

½ teaspoon cream of tartar

½ teaspoon vanilla extract

¼ teaspoon kosher salt

LEMON CURD:

⅔ cup granulated sugar

2 tablespoons grated lemon zest

½ cup fresh lemon juice

½ teaspoon kosher salt

5 large egg yolks

½ cup (1 stick) unsalted butter, cubed

FOR GARNISH:

¼ cup shelled pistachios, chopped

1. Preheat the oven to 225°F.

2. Make the meringue: In the scrupulously clean bowl of a stand mixer fitted with the whisk attachment, whip the egg whites on medium-low speed. When they have doubled in volume, slowly add ½ cup of the superfine sugar a tablespoon at a time.

3. Increase the speed to medium and add the cream of tartar, vanilla, and salt. Scrape down the sides and add the rest of the sugar a tablespoon at a time until the whites form stiff peaks and are shiny.

4. Using a large soup spoon, scoop up about a cup of the meringue and place on a baking sheet, forming a dollop. Make a large dimple in the middle. Repeat with the rest of the meringue, making 6 dollops.

5. Bake for 1 hour, then kill the heat. Do not open the door. Let the meringues rest in the oven for another hour. Now crack the door open with a wooden spoon and let cool for another hour.

6. Make the lemon curd: In a small saucepan over low heat, whisk together the sugar, lemon zest, lemon juice, salt, and egg yolks. Continue whisking until smooth, then add the butter cubes, one at a time. The goal is to softly cook the yolks without breaking them. Stay on low heat and continue to whisk; after 6 to 8 minutes, the curd should start to thicken.

7. When the curd coats the back of a spoon, pour it into a heatproof bowl. Let cool, then place in the refrigerator to chill.

8. To serve, place a meringue on a plate, fill the dimple with the chilled curd, and garnish with the chopped pistachios.

This recipe will give you a light, crispy meringue. If you want it to be a little chewy in the middle, shave 15 minutes off the bake time and 30 minutes off the rest time.

Real espresso is a must here because tiramisu needs the decadent chocolate notes you get from good espresso. If you don't have an espresso machine at home, visit your local barista and order some up for takeaway.

This no-bake recipe uses raw egg yolks, so be sure to use farm-fresh pastured eggs; if you're not comfortable using raw eggs, you can use pasteurized eggs instead.

If you can't finish it all, you can store leftover tiramisu in the refrigerator for up to a week.

TIRAMISU

YIELD: 4 TO 6 SERVINGS · PREP TIME: 15 MINUTES, PLUS 2 HOURS TO CHILL

Tiramisu is such a classic dessert. However, we never knew how much we loved it until we took our first trip to Barcelona together and ordered it off the dessert menu at Bar Cañete. Let's just say that it's one of the tastiest desserts, and in this version it's made even tastier yet with a luxurious topping of softly whipped cream and mascarpone that cascades down the sides, enveloping every inch of it. But man, it's so ugly to look at. Like all relationships, though, there's more (much more) than meets the eye. Don't let appearances fool you; this one's got the goods for a truly happy ending.

3 tablespoons granulated sugar

6 large egg yolks

1½ cups espresso, room temperature, divided

16 ounces mascarpone

1 ounce dark rum

24 lady fingers (about one 13-ounce package)

½ cup heavy cream

1 tablespoon powdered sugar

1 tablespoon cocoa powder, for dusting

1. In a stand mixer fitted with the whisk attachment, whisk the sugar and egg yolks on medium-high speed until frothy. Add 1 teaspoon of the espresso and the mascarpone and whisk on medium speed until smooth. Scoop out ¼ cup of the mascarpone mixture for the whipped cream topping and place in the refrigerator until needed.

2. Pour the remaining espresso into a medium bowl and add the rum. (Why not have a shot of rum yourself while you're at it?)

3. Dip half of the lady fingers into the espresso and rum mixture and arrange in a 9 by 13-inch baking pan.

4. Top with about half of the mascarpone mixture, then repeat with the remaining lady fingers, espresso mixture, and mascarpone mixture to make two layers.

5. Chill for 2 hours, then cut into portions and plate.

6. Using a metal bowl and a hand whisk so that you don't overmix, whip the cream and powdered sugar until soft peaks form. Fold in the reserved mascarpone mixture and dollop over each portion of tiramisu.

7. Garnish with the cocoa powder and serve.

RECIPE INDEX

BREAK THE ICE

Limoncello Mint Spritz

The Pimm's Cup

Cilantro Jalapeño Maple
Tequila on the Rocks

Katherine's Caesar

Espresso Martini

Frozen Peach Bellini

Pear and Plum
White Sangria

Frozen Avocado
Margarita

Oyster Shooter

FIRST DATE

Oysters Rockefeller

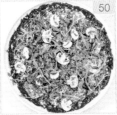
Beef Carpaccio

Seared Sea Scallops with Celeriac Puree and Crispy Guanciale

Burrata Arancini

Beet-Cured Gravlax

Curly Endive and Apple Salad with Goat Cheese Crème Brûlée

Cream of Mushroom Soup

Crispy Rosemary Chicken Wings with Honey Hot Sauce

Green Coconut Curry Mussels

MORNING GLORY

Vanilla Coffee Syrup

Homemade Granola with Yogurt, Mint, and Black Pepper

Eggs Benedict

Eggs with Soldiers

Crispy Feta Egg

Katherine's Perfect Lox Bagel

Ham and Brie Croissant Pudding

Leek and Asparagus Quiche

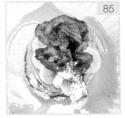
Nutella French Toast

Oscar's Smoked Salmon and Potato Rosti

QUICKIES

Crab Cakes

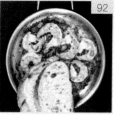

Gambas al Ajilo (Spanish-Style Garlic Shrimp)

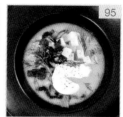

Kulajda (Czech Mushroom Soup)

Muffuletta

Rapini Linguine with Burrata

Lamb Meatballs with Mint Tzatziki

Blue Cheese Mushroom Toast

Heirloom Tomato Salad

Bikini Ham and Cheese

MEET THE PARENTS

Rosé Grilled Oysters

Prime Rib au Jus

Maple Syrup Smoked Salmon

Sumac Porchetta

Three-Cheese Chicken Parmigiana

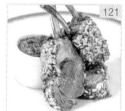

Pistachio Chive–Crusted Rack of Lamb with Mint Sauce

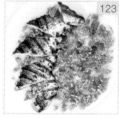

Crispy Mackerel with Vierge Sauce

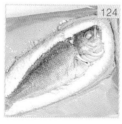

Salt-Baked Snapper

Tartiflette

GOING STEADY

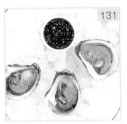
Oysters Mignonette

Coconut Poached Cod

Charred Octopus

Beef Tartare

Roasted Red Pepper and
Feta Soup

Cheese Fondue

Spicy Vodka Penne

Golden Beet Carpaccio

Kartöffelchen

MARRY ME SALADS

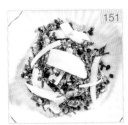
Gusto's Kale Salad

Ten-Vegetable Slaw with
Peanut-Lime Dressing

Curly Endive with
Mashed Potato
Vinaigrette

Peach and Endive Salad
for Two

Ranch Iceberg
Wedge Salad

Panzanella with
Charred Green Onions

Tarragon Mustard
Citrus Salad

Big Salad, Little Steak

Lentil, Feta, and
Parsley Salad

GROWING OLD TOGETHER

Boeuf Bourguignon

Chicken Pernod

Cheese Drawer Risotto
with Sun-Dried Tomato
Pesto

Cauliflower Chicken
Pot Pie

Red Wine–Braised
Short Ribs

Meatballs with Polenta

Squid Puttanesca

Spatchcocked Roast
Chicken with Salsa Verde

GET OUT OF JAIL FREE CARD

Wine and Cheese

Squid Sandwich

French Onion
Soup-Sandwich

Seared Foie Gras and
Vanilla Poached Pear

Caviar Pizza Fritta

Blood Orange Scallop
Crudo

King Crab with Clarified
Chili-Garlic Butter

Spaghetti Carbonara

Randy Bo Bandy
Cheeseburger

BY YOUR SIDE

Cheddar Jalapeño
Creamed Corn

Charred Zucchini
Romesco

Rapini and Leek with
Cannellini Beans

Turmeric Maple Syrup
Roasted Carrots

Asparagus Salad with
Whipped Goat Cheese
and Harissa Hazelnuts

Irish Brown Soda Bread

Potato Colcannon

One-Pan Smashed
Potatoes

Creamy Peppercorn
Sauce

HAPPY ENDINGS

Vanilla Bean Soft-Serve

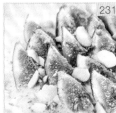
Brûléed Figs with
Sabayon

Burnt Cheesecake

Olive Oil Chocolate Tart

Coconut Cream Pie

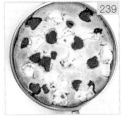
Raspberry Cream
Cheese Cobbler

Chocolate Maple
Brown Butter Cookies

Sticky Toffee Pudding

Meringue with
Lemon Curd

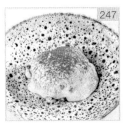
Tiramisu

GENERAL INDEX

harissa
   Asparagus Salad with Whipped
      Goat Cheese and Harissa
      Hazelnuts, 216–217
   Lamb Meatballs with Tzatziki,
      100–101
hazelnut cocoa spread
   Nutella French Toast, 84–85
hazelnuts
   Asparagus Salad with Whipped
      Goat Cheese and Harissa
      Hazelnuts, 216–217
heavy cream
   Burnt Cheesecake, 232–233
   Cheddar Jalapeño Creamed
      Corn, 208–209
   Crab Cakes, 90–91
   Cream of Mushroom Soup,
      60–61
   Creamy Peppercorn Sauce,
      224–225
   Kulajda (Czech-Style Mushroom
      Soup), 94–95
   Leek and Asparagus Quiche,
      82–83
   Olive Oil Chocolate Tart, 234–235
   Potato Colcannon, 220–221
   Spicy Vodka Penne, 142–143
   Sticky Toffee Pudding, 242–243
   Tiramisu, 246–247
   Vanilla Bean Soft-Serve, 228–229
Heirloom Tomato Salad, 104–105
heirloom tomatoes
   Heirloom Tomato Salad, 104–105
   Panzanella with Charred Green
      Onions, 160–161
   purchasing, 160
herb oil, 138–139
hollandaise, 72–73
Homemade Cold-Smoked Salmon
   Katherine's Perfect Lox Bagel,
      78–79
Homemade Granola with Yogurt, Mint
   and Black Pepper, 70–71
honey
   Crispy Rosemary Chicken Wings
      with Honey Hot Sauce, 62–63
horseradish
   Prime Rib au Jus, 112–113
hot sauce
   Katherine's Caesar, 34–35
   Oyster Shooter, 44–45

I

ice cream
   Raspberry Cream Cheese
      Cobbler, 238–239
   Sticky Toffee Pudding, 242–243
   Vanilla Bean Soft-Serve, 228–229

iceberg lettuce
   Ranch Iceberg Wedge Salad,
      158–159
ingredients, staple, 21–23
Irish Brown Soda Bread, 218–219

J–K

jalapeño peppers
   Blood Orange Scallop Crudo,
      198–199
   Cheddar Jalapeño Creamed
      Corn, 208–209
   Cilantro Jalapeño Maple Tequila
      on the Rocks, 32–33
   Oyster Shooter, 44–45
kaffir lime leaves
   Coconut Poached Cod, 132–133
kale
   Gusto's Kale Salad, 150–151
Kartöffelchen, 146–147
Katherine Wants brand, 7, 9
Katherine's Caesar, 34–35
Katherine's Perfect Lox Bagel, 78–79
kefir
   Ranch Iceberg Wedge Salad,
      158–159
King Crab with Clarified Chili-Garlic
   Butter, 200–201
Kirsch
   Cheese Fondue, 140–141
kitchen staples, 21–25
kitchen torch, 58
kosher salt
   Salt-Baked Snapper, 124–125
Kulajda (Czech-Style Mushroom
   Soup), 94–95

L

lady fingers
   Tiramisu, 246–247
lamb
   Crispy Feta Egg, 76–77
   Lamb Meatballs with Tzatziki,
      100–101
Lamb Meatballs with Tzatziki,
   100–101
lamb stock
   Lamb Meatballs with Tzatziki,
      100–101
lardons
   bacon, 126–127, 170–171
   guanciale, 202–203
Leek and Asparagus Quiche, 82–83
leeks
   Leek and Asparagus Quiche,
      82–83
   Rapini and Leek with Cannellini
      Beans, 212–213
   washing, 213

lemongrass
   Coconut Poached Cod, 132–133
lemons/lemon juice
   Asparagus Salad with Whipped
      Goat Cheese and Harissa
      Hazelnuts, 216–217
   Beef Carpaccio, 50–51
   Beef Tartare, 136–137
   Brûléed Figs with Sabayon,
      230–231
   Charred Octopus, 134–135
   Cheese Drawer Risotto with Sun-
      Dried Tomato Pesto, 174–175
   Cheese Fondue, 140–141
   Crab Cakes, 90–91
   Crispy Mackerel with Vierge
      Sauce, 122–123
   Curly Endive and Apple Salad
      with Goat Cheese Crème
      Brûlée, 58–59
   Eggs Benedict, 72–73
   Gambas al Ajilo (Spanish-Style
      Garlic Shrimp), 92–93
   Gusto's Kale Salad, 150–151
   Katherine's Caesar, 34–35
   Katherine's Perfect Lox Bagel,
      78–79
   Lamb Meatballs with Tzatziki,
      100–101
   Lentil, Feta and Parsley Salad,
      166–167
   Limoncello Mint Spritz, 28–29
   Maple Syrup Smoked Salmon,
      114–115
   Meringue with Lemon Curd,
      244–245
   Muffuletta, 96–97
   One-Pan Smashed Potatoes,
      222–223
   Oyster Shooter, 44–45
   Oysters Rockefeller, 48–49
   Peach and Endive Salad for Two,
      156–157
   The Pimm's Cup, 30–31
   Ranch Iceberg Wedge Salad,
      158–159
   Rapini Linguine with Burrata,
      98–99
   Raspberry Cream Cheese
      Cobbler, 238–239
   Roasted Red Pepper and Feta
      Soup, 138–139
   Rosé Grilled Oysters, 110–111
   Salt-Baked Snapper, 124–125
   Squid Sandwich, 190–191
   Turmeric Maple Syrup Roasted
      Carrots, 214–215
Lentil, Feta and Parsley Salad,
   166–167